PLAYFUL
SELF-DISCOVERY

Other works by David Earl Platts

International Psychosynthesis Directory

Works with Eileen Caddy

Books

Bringing More Love Into Your Life: The Choice Is Yours

Choosing To Love

Opening Doors Within

Audio Tapes

Be Still: Meditation For the Child Within

The Challenge of Change

Loving Unconditionally

Why Meditate?

These works may be ordered from Findhorn Press

PLAYFUL
SELF-DISCOVERY

A Findhorn Foundation Approach
To Building Trust in Groups

David Earl Platts, Ph.D.

FINDHORN
Press

ISBN 1-899171-06-1

British Library Cataloguing-in-Publication Data.
A catalogue record for this book is available
from the British Library.

'Learning to See Each Other' adapted from
Despair and Personal Power In The Nuclear Age,
by Joanna Rogers Macy, Ph.D., ISBN 0-86571-031-7,
used by permission of the author.

'Evocation of Openness' and 'What I Love About Myself' from
Bringing More Love Into Your Life: The Choice Is Yours,
by Eileen Caddy and David Earl Platts, Ph.D.,
ISBN 0-905249-75-5, used by permission of the authors.

Cover illustration by Simon Hepple
Cover design by David Gregson
Author's photograph by Ron Parker
Layout and setting in Garamond by Findhorn Press
Printed and bound by Cromwell Press Ltd., Melksham, England

Published by
Findhorn Press
The Park, Findhorn,
Forres IV36 0TZ, Scotland
01309-690582/fax 690036
e-mail thierry@findhorn.org
http://www.gaia.org/findhornpress/

CONTENTS

This book is dedicated affectionately
to everyone who has ever facilitated or taken part in
a *Group Discovery* session at the Findhorn Foundation.

ACKNOWLEDGEMENTS

Playful Self-Discovery (or *Group Discovery* as it is called at the Findhorn Foundation), has a history going back more than 20 years, and many people have played an important part in its development.

I am pleased to recognise my friends and former colleagues Joy Drake, Mary Inglis, Alexis Edwards Lauren and other members of the Findhorn Foundation education department who first breathed life into the concept of using exercises and games to build trust in groups.

Then Stewart Brand, Andrew Fluegelman, Dale LeFevre, Terry Orlick and Shoshana Tembeck began collecting, creating and publishing new games which contributed to the evolving process of using games for a purpose embracing, yet going beyond their recreational value.

I thank Hilary McKay Martin for asking me in the early 1980s to take over *Group Discovery,* as it led to my creating for the 'Experience Week' and other guest workshops a formalised strategy and structure which are still in place today. I also thank all the subsequent facilitators who have honoured the strategy and structure and kept them pure.

I wish to express deep gratitude to my friends Eileen Caddy and Patricia Russell for the solid encouragement, love and support they have given me throughout the years, and most especially during the last few challenging months it has taken to complete this book.

Other friends are Thierry and Karin Bogliolo who, as publishers of Findhorn Press, were quick to see the book's value and, together with Sandra Kramer and her consummate skills as editor and designer, have fashioned an original idea into an attractive and usable book.

I also appreciate and thank my partner Lorna M. Richardson for her helpful suggestions, profound and abiding love, strength, courage and understanding during the year this book has been in process.

The exercises and games selected for use in *Playful Self-Discovery* have been around for a long time and have evolved from within the Findhorn Foundation, the international psychosynthesis community and the consciousness movement at large. The original source has been credited when. it was known. If unintentionally other people have been overlooked, I would be grateful if they would come forward to be acknowledged in subsequent editions.

FOREWORD

by Eileen Caddy

I do hope you enjoy the session of exercises and games described in this book as much as I have done over the years.

David Earl Platts and I have presented many workshops together, and we have always used these games with our groups. We have found them a wonderful way of bringing a group together through play, fun and laughter, and of helping many people who have not found coming close to others an easy thing to do.

I have seen how the *Playful Self-Discovery* session changes people, how it opens their hearts and helps them to come together in a most amazing way. It is a miracle well worth experiencing to watch a group of people at the beginning of a session, and to wonder how these games are going to bring them together, and then, as time flies by, to see the joy, love and peace come alive in them. Time and again I have witnessed how the session is a deeply moving and powerful experience for many people, often the highlight of their stay at the Findhorn Foundation.

I had an experience I shall never forget when I was taking part in one of these sessions. In one exercise, 'Learning to See Each Other', we had to sit in front of partners and look into their eyes for several minutes. I was shy and embarrassed, and besides, the person who chose me was the last person I wanted to do it with. As the minutes ticked by, I began to see beyond the physical person to a very beautiful soul, and by the end of the exercise, we were both in tears. It was a very good reminder never to judge anyone by outer appearances.

As well as giving workshops together, David and I are co-authors of several tapes and books, and so I know how creatively and professionally he handles everything he does and also how very caring and loving he is. For many years, David also focalised *Group Discovery* at the Findhorn Foundation, learning a great deal about the method and how it works and becoming expert at facilitating sessions.

For all these reasons I thoroughly recommend both this book and David Earl Platts who gives workshops and trainings on the

Playful Self-Discovery method and other personal development topics.

Have fun and enjoy yourself, either leading a session of exercises and games, or being part of a group participating in them. You won't be the same person when you have finished. You will find yourself more open, free and joyous.

GROUP DISCOVERY
THE EARLY DAYS

by Mary Inglis

Soon after I first came to the Findhorn Foundation, Alexis Edwards, a community member who was an actor, began doing a series of theatre games as part of the winter of 1973 study programme for members. This was the beginning of what was later to become *Group Discovery* — so-called because participants discovered things about interacting with other members of a group, finding their own part in the whole while having an awareness and appreciation of what other people were doing, and discovering more about creativity and spontaneity, often in an improvisational way.

Shortly afterwards a group of us who either had been involved with different kinds of group and personal development work, or who were interested in it, got together for a week to share our knowledge and experience, and see what we could create and develop together that would be appropriate here. It was a rich and deep week, filled with communication exercises, gestalt and fantasy work, visualisations, some physical and emotional work, interactive group exercises, theatre games, leadership training exercises and some games we played just for the fun of it or that emerged spontaneously from the group. Out of this week together, a smaller group developed which began designing experiential group sessions for the membership, often for particular work departments, lasting anything from an afternoon to a full day.

Then we started using the exercises and games in our programmes for guests. In the 'Experience Week' programme we did an experiential section towards the beginning of the week, geared to the guests getting to know themselves and each other better. This kind of approach to learning and interaction was still fairly new, not just in the Foundation but also in the culture at large. Sometimes the look on guests' faces was quite amusing when they first realised we were going to play games, but the guests soon engaged with them and got a lot of value from them.

The sessions helped people open to themselves and each other on a deeper level than ordinary conversation or discussion would have done, and usually bonded the group quite deeply, helping to create a support system that lasted throughout the week and often beyond.

One exercise we frequently used involved participants choosing an object from nature and then describing themselves as this object. Often a lot of feeling and insight would come up for people as they did it. I remember an older woman who chose a beautiful but fragile flower. As she brought it into the room the petals started to fall off. She began to describe herself as this flower, coming to the end of her life, with the things she had achieved beginning to fall away. Now she was fading, and she felt that the beauty of the flower had never really been seen and appreciated. Now, with the petals gone, it never would be. The whole group were with her as she connected with and shared her grief at feeling she had not lived fully and that so few people had seen her beauty. But as she opened to herself and to the support of the group, she found something strong within herself. It was a very important experience for her, though an uncomfortable one. She was seen by the group that week, and was able to celebrate both who she was and who she had been. And everyone experienced her beauty.

In the early days *Group Discovery* was not regarded as very important by many people in the Foundation — maybe because it seemed playful and often lighthearted in comparison to the more theoretical and physical work — so there was initially some resistance to making it part of our 'formal' educational work. Two breakthrough points helped it become more established. One was a morning of experiential games and exercises we offered during the first conference at Cluny Hill, on Transpersonal Psychology, which most participants — many of them 'serious' psychologists — loved. The other was when the Foundation started ed a College, and we did a full week of *Group Discovery* with the students focusing on group-building, trust, creativity, spontaneity, and self-exploration and self-knowledge; it proved an important contribution to their programme.

A number of different approaches to personal and transpersonal growth were coming into the community at that time, including Psychosynthesis, Re-evaluation Counselling, Bio-energetics, and Rebirthing, and we began incorporating aspects of these approaches into what we were offering. We created many new exercises, and designed specific sessions for workshops with particular themes. Many of the workshops offered to the public in the early days had a lot of theoretical input and discussion, and we argued strongly for more experiential work to support the theory and allow it to be explored in a different way. What we could offer became more substantial, and *Group Discovery* itself became a tool for self-discovery, group interaction, exploring different parts of oneself, developing interpersonal skills, deepening trust and creating community. As the interest in it increased, we began training people to facilitate the games and exercises for guest groups, as well as for the more specialised programmes. And so it developed to what it is today, an integral part of many of our programmes.

It was all very creative and playful and light in the early days. Not non-serious, but light. From what I can tell, it still is.

INTRODUCTION

This book describes a unique method of building trust in both new and established groups. Since 1974 it has been used regularly with great success for thousands of guests who visit the Findhorn Foundation each year to participate in its educational programme of short courses and conferences.

The method is deceptively simple and complex. It functions on two primary levels. First, on an *individual* level, it provides sessions of light-hearted games and exercises designed to give participants insight into their own attitudes, beliefs and patterns of behaviour, such as how the issues of trust and openness function (or fail to function) in their lives.

In an atmosphere free of evaluation and judgment, the sessions also encourage spontaneous play, and the consequent letting go of the need to try to control events in one's life, itself a formidable barrier to trust and openness.

Many of the activities are action-oriented and require few or no words to perform, aside from initial instructions. In Findhorn Foundation terms, these activities are chosen 'to lead the participants out of their heads and into their bodies and feelings'.

Later in the session, other activities take participants deeper inside themselves to explore their inner world. All of these activities are tailored specifically to each group and are chosen carefully and sequenced strategically to help participants to set aside the inhibitions which prevent them from relating more freely and fully to others.

Second, on a *group* level, the method fosters authentic human contact among group members. Following the sessions, the group *as a group* begins to form a character of its own, demonstrating more open communication, cooperation, acceptance, trust and awareness.

Rather than being a fragmented collection of isolated individuals, the group becomes more cohesive and discovers, paradoxically, a sense of unity in the midst of its own diversity. Goodwill increases and group dynamics are enhanced. As a result, a collective group consciousness begins to emerge, and the group functions more effectively, whatever its purpose and responsibilities may be.

These transformative changes can come quite quickly when the group has been properly prepared and is sufficiently open and ready for the experience.

It must be emphasised that *Playful Self-Discovery* needs to be integrated as part of an overall process and general policy of building and maintaining trust in groups if its effects are to be long lasting.

A word of caution. *Playful Self-Discovery* is not a panacea or magic wand for groups with difficulties in communication, morale, personal relationships and so on. But it can open a door to the resolution of such difficulties for those groups able to work on themselves in an atmosphere of goodwill and shared values.

This book comes from my personal experience as a staff member in the Findhorn Foundation education department, in charge of its *Group Discovery* programme for many years, training, scheduling and supervising new facilitators and writing a step-by-step training manual upon which this book is based.

The first part of the book provides detailed guidelines under three headings: 'Preparing the Group', 'Planning the Session' and 'Presenting the Session'. The second part presents complete word-for-word instructions to 67 exercises and games which may be used in a *Playful Self-Discovery* session or in the 'Preparation Session' which precedes it.

Feedback about your experience with this book and the sessions it describes is welcome. Address all correspondence care of Findhorn Press, The Park, Findhorn, Forres IV36 0TZ, Scotland.

David Earl Platts, Ph.D.
February 19, 1996
London

GUIDELINES

GUIDELINES

Purpose

The term *Playful Self-Discovery* refers to a diverse collection of new games, psychosynthesis exercises, guided imageries and other related creative activities used systematically to bring groups together. For new groups at the Findhorn Foundation where it is known as *Group Discovery,* it is usually scheduled for the third day of a seven-day residential course.

Playful Self-Discovery is also effective with established groups which have been together for a while and which are ongoing and open-ended, such as athletic groups, business groups, hobby groups, religious groups, special interest groups, study groups, work groups and so on.

The only requirements necessary to obtain successful results from *Playful Self-Discovery* are for all participants to have basic goodwill towards each other and the group, and to hold a positive common intention (vision or purpose) for the group.

A word of caution about attitude. If some people in a group are openly resistant, rebellious or disruptive (perhaps because they are attending the session involuntarily or because they have hidden grievances or motivations), their negativity can seriously affect the outcome. To derive optimal benefits from a session, everyone needs to have a positive attitude towards it.

For all its lightness, *Playful Self-Discovery* is a serious business. It is more than simply introducing people to each other or helping them to have recreational fun. Most participants generally do have a good time in the session, but the prospective session facilitator is advised to distinguish the means from the ends.

The primary purposes of *Playful Self-Discovery* are to build trust and openness in a group, to help it come together as a group and to give participants a conscious experience of their identity as a group. These tasks are accomplished by seeking to break through barriers to open and honest communication among participants so they may accept each other as warm, loving human beings, in short, what is sometimes called establishing 'heart connections' with one another.

For this important shift to occur, it is essential that as a *Playful Self-Discovery* facilitator you work diligently (by modelling a good example) to create a totally open, safe and secure atmosphere for all participants, free from evaluation and judgment. Your task is simply to encourage people to open themselves to one another gently, safely and lovingly.

Facilitation not Manipulation

Care needs to be taken when reading and applying the guidelines presented in this book. They are suggestions intended to help *facilitate* a group, and not to *manipulate* it as beginning facilitators sometimes suppose.

Actually, facilitation and manipulation are two completely different processes.

Manipulation in its derogatory sense . . .

1. *Makes* something happen and therefore imposes force, power, domination or control
2. Wants a specific outcome and is determined to get it
3. Focuses primarily on the means to achieve the desired outcome
4. Regards people as objects to be influenced, exploited or controlled

Facilitation within the context of this book . . .

1. *Helps, supports* and *allows* something to happen
2. Accepts any outcome as valid, useful and worthwhile
3. Focuses primarily on people and their needs
4. Respects people and accepts them as they are

As a beginning *Playful Self-Discovery* facilitator, please hold these distinctions clearly in mind as you read through the following guidelines and as you prepare and present sessions for groups.

PREPARING THE GROUP

As has been pointed out, to obtain beneficial results from *Playful Self-Discovery* all participants need to have basic goodwill towards each other and to hold a positive common intention for the group.

A preparatory stage is often needed (especially for newly-formed groups) to create sufficient safety and trust to foster this goodwill and common intention. Basically, participants need to spend enough time together to feel generally at ease with each other before *Playful Self-Discovery* can be introduced. For many groups, this process may take only a few hours.

Such preparation is usually easier with newly-formed groups as fewer given circumstances have to be accommodated, whereas with established, ongoing groups, challenging personal dynamics such as biases, conflicts, fears, grudges, hurts, jealousies, resentments and so on may require attention *before* real trust can be built.

Otherwise, in a session some participants may only go through the motions, become silent saboteurs, or even be overtly disruptive, and in so doing hold the group back in its development. Confronting and resolving difficult group dynamics and inter-relationship issues to everyone's satisfaction is the worthy subject for another book.

Suffice it to say here that the *Playful Self-Discovery* facilitator needs to learn as much as possible about an established group before planning a session, and perhaps even before agreeing to present a session.

The author finds the following four-hour format, designed for a newly-formed group, usually sufficient to prepare people adequately for *Playful Self-Discovery*, if they are all basically open and receptive to taking part. This 'Preparation Session' may be scheduled either in the afternoon before a *Playful Self-Discovery* session is presented the following morning, or in the morning before a session in the afternoon.

Note that listing clock times in the outline allows you to monitor your progress during the session and make adjustments as you go along if necessary.

PREPARATION SESSION

Starting Time	Activity

9.00 WELCOME AND OVERVIEW (15 minutes)
This introduction to the day helps participants to settle into the group and to begin to feel comfortable with the facilitator. It may include a general summary of the schedule as well as administrative and other logistical details. Participants are invited to stay in touch with their feelings and their experience of the group.

9.15 ICE-BREAKER (15 minutes)
Participants begin to relax as they become aware of who everyone is by meeting and greeting each other briefly. Refer to 'Ice-Breaker', page 90, for instructions.

9.30 ALLY EXERCISE (15 minutes)
This exercise gives participants an 'ally', that is, someone to connect and feel comfortable with. This exercise may also be used to set up the 'Personal Introductions' which follow. Refer to 'Ally Exercise', page 45, for instructions.

9.45 PERSONAL INTRODUCTIONS (2 hours)
Participants have five minutes each to introduce themselves to the group. They are encouraged to be open and to take risks in what they disclose about themselves, and thus they begin to create a trusting atmosphere. Refer to 'Personal Introductions', page 105, for instructions.

11.00 REFRESHMENT BREAK (30 minutes)
This extended intermission provides time for participants to continue to make contact with each other.

11.30	PERSONAL INTRODUCTIONS RESUME

12.15   GROUP AGREEMENTS (15 minutes)
Participants are invited to specify and agree upon conditions under which they would like the group to function, and thus create additional safety and trust for themselves. Refer to 'Group Agreements', page 79, for instructions.

12.30   EXPECTATIONS (15 minutes)
Participants identify and begin to release the hopes and fears they have about the group to allow them to relax and be fully present. Refer to 'Expectations', page 71, for instructions.

12.45   INTRODUCTION TO THE *PLAYFUL SELF-DISCOVERY* SESSION (15 minutes)
The facilitator directly addresses the session by providing information and answering questions. Refer to 'Presenting Instructions for the Game', page 32, to determine which points may be made at this time and which may be made (or repeated) at the beginning of the actual session.

Include the following point, "As you will be doing some dancing and running about, and maybe even sitting or lying on the floor at times, dress comfortably. Jeans, loose-fitting clothes and trainers are definitely recommended."

Depending on the nature and purpose of the group, the facilitator may wish to present the *Playful Self-Discovery* session within the context of Team Building, Stress Management, Group Dynamics, Group Consciousness or other business or organisational themes, as well as fostering the qualities of trust and openness.

1.00   COMPLETION

PLANNING THE SESSION

Working with a Co-Facilitator or Alone

Once you have decided to facilitate a *Playful Self-Discovery* session, then decide if you wish to lead the session with another person or by yourself. For many years at the Findhorn Foundation, two people shared the responsibilities equally, and this practice is preferable for the obvious advantages it offers to you and to the group:

● A co-facilitator gives the group a second person to relate to, and participants often naturally relate more easily to one than the other.

● A co-facilitator is useful in demonstrating exercises and games.

● A co-facilitator helps to get equipment ready, cue up audio tapes, distribute materials and so on.

● A co-facilitator is a help in games which require participants to work in twos or threes, as an additional person may be needed to participate to make the numbers come out right, and it is preferable if one facilitator remains entirely free to lead a game and to hold the awareness for the entire group.

● A co-facilitator can do whatever is needed in the unlikely event someone becomes ill or injured during the session.

● A co-facilitator, while another person is leading a game, is free to observe participants more closely (for example, noticing which participants have trouble keeping their eyes closed during trust games, which participants seem to need to be in control, which of them use humour or other defence mechanisms to keep participants or the entire experience safely at arm's length, and so on.) Once observed, such group members may subsequently be given additional encouragement and support by the facilitators during the refreshment break or following the session.

These benefits notwithstanding, it is also entirely possible for you to lead the session by yourself. The author has done it for years as a matter of necessity, but being the sole facilitator requires even greater attention than usual to careful planning and presenting.

The Group

The preferable group size for *Playful Self-Discovery* is between 12 and 24 participants. While groups smaller than 12 may benefit, the session needs to be modified because certain exercises and games require a minimum of a dozen participants or so (for example, 'Lap Sit'). Likewise, adaptation of some games is necessary for groups of more than 24 participants. Obviously, the larger the group, the greater the need for your close attention and the greater the challenge to help the group to come together as a cohesive whole. Therefore the session described in this book is recommended for groups of no more than 30 participants.

Before you begin planning the session, check these factors as they may influence the exercises and games you choose as well as your general approach to the group.

- Size of the group
- Age range of participants
- People who may have some difficulty with the language
- People who may have a disability, for example, who have hearing or vision problems, or who use canes, wheelchairs and so on.

The Time

The standard *Playful Self-Discovery* format consists of a four-hour session. (Findhorn Foundation course participants receive considerable ongoing support and reinforcement in a residential setting for one week or longer, and therefore their *Playful Self-Discovery* sessions are usually three hours in length.) Once you are experienced and comfortable with the basic format, feel free to facilitate sessions of varying length. For example, the author presents *Playful Self-Discovery* sessions, general courses and facilitator trainings six hours a day lasting from one to seven days.

If you want to achieve effective results, lead sessions of at least *four full hours.* The *Playful Self-Discovery* process takes time to unfold, that is, to work within the individual participants and within the group as a whole, and accordingly it should not be hurried or cut short.

The Venue

Proper room size and ambience are critical factors for the success of the session. For 12-24 participants, choose a square-shaped room at least 10 x 10 metres, with no furniture (or with furniture which may be moved completely out of the room) and no support columns in the middle of the room to restrict vision and movement.

The room needs adequate lighting, fresh air ventilation and central heating capable of providing a uniform comfortable temperature. The floor, which may be carpeted or not, needs to be quite clean as participants sit and lie upon it. If possible, choose a room which is neutral and new to participants (not one which is on their own home ground, such as their work place) to provide a fresh experience.

Always hold the session indoors, no matter how tempting the weather and the setting may be. Otherwise, participants often have trouble hearing (over the noise of lawn mowers, traffic, aeroplanes and other ambient sound), find grass awkward to dance on and run through, are distracted or annoyed by insects and stray animals and generally contribute to the group focus of attention being dispersed rather than consolidated.

The Session Format

The typical *Playful Self-Discovery* session is divided into two parts, usually separated by a refreshment break. The first part focuses largely on physical activity with several short, action-oriented, non-verbal games. Such contact activities as 'Hug Tag', 'People-to-People', 'Group Knot' and 'Shoulder Massage' require participants to touch each other physically, a necessary preparation which lays the ground work for the introspective, more vulnerable part to follow after the break.

The second part features fewer, quieter, longer games which help participants experience their feelings, explore aspects of their own inner life and express them safely to others in the group, thus encouraging emotional and intellectual closeness as well. By quickly establishing an atmosphere of safety, intimacy and trust *on all levels, Playful Self-Discovery* helps a 'collection of individuals' begin to coalesce into a more cohesive group within a matter of hours.

Planning Session

In a planning session, either on your own, or with your co-facilitator:

1. Plan to go more deeply more quickly if a group has been together for a long time and is comfortable with itself.

2. Decide if there is to be a theme for the group, for example, communication, health, relationships, synthesis, trust, etc.

3. Decide on an outline of exercises and games, the time allotment for each and their sequence.

Although groups vary widely in their size, composition, and purpose, a general strategy and structure for planning *any Playful Self-Discovery* session have evolved over the years, summarised in the following step-by-step sequence of games. Refer also to Chart 1, pages 124-125, for a complete listing of exercises and games by primary type.

● *Opening Games.* To bring the group together as a group at the very beginning of the session (Greeting Dance, Name Chain, Name Mantra, Pillow Toss).

● *Name Games.* To help participants learn each other's names, begin to make contact with each other and become more relaxed (Ice-Breaker, Name Chain, Name Mantra, Nicknames, Pillow Toss).

● *Action Games.* To promote vigorous activity, to loosen up, to warm up and to discharge tensions physically and vocally (Everybody Is It, Frozen Tag, Head, Shoulders, Knees and Toes, Hug Tag, Sentence Completion).

● *Silly Games.* To continue the physical release and to break through personal reserve (Caterpillar, Circle Pass, Cows and Ducks, Elephants' Scratch, Energy Creation, Everybody Is It, Fairies and Dragons, Frozen Tag, Head, Shoulders, Knees and Toes, Hug Tag, Humless, Morning Routine, People-to-People, Prui, Sentence Completion).

● *Creative Games.* To encourage individual expression of imagination and creativity (Choosing A Leader, Energy Creation, Group Story, Mirroring, Morning Routine, Moving Statues, Picture Post Cards).

● *Trust Games.* To help participants observe how trust works in their lives and to begin to open themselves to each other. All eyes-closed games are trust games. (Blind Sculptor, Camera Walk, Car-Car, Car Wash, Cows and Ducks, Cradle Rock, Cup Massage, Elephant Walk, Hand-to-Hand Communication, Human Spring, Humless, Lap Sit, People Pass, Planets, Prui, Sensuality Walk, Shoulder Massage, Stand Up, Trust Fall, Trust Walk).

● *Close-Touching Games.* A continuation of trust games which prompt touching physically in non-threatening ways. (Blind Sculptor, Car-Car, Car Wash, Caterpillar, Cradle Rock, Cup Massage, Elephants' Scratch, Group Knot, Group Spiral, Lap Sit, People Pass, People-to-People, Shoulder Massage, Trust Fall, Unfolding).

● *Refreshment Break.* To ground and integrate participants' experience of the first half of the session and to foster their making continued, authentic contact with each other. Thus, if possible, it is preferable for everyone to stay together as a group in the same general location for this important grounding and integration to take place.

● *Self-Exploration/Revelation Games.* To enable participants to learn more about themselves and each other, and to talk about their learning openly to each other (Animal Identification, Camera Walk, Choosing A Leader, Creating Your Own Reality, Evocation of Openness, Eye Contact, Fairies and Dragons, Fountain of Love, Learning to See Each Other, Free Association, Nicknames, Picture Post Cards, Sensuality Walk, What I Love About Myself, What is Your Next Step?).

● *Attunement and Caring Games.* To help participants to attune to each other and to the group, and to give and receive warmth and caring. In its simplest form, attunement is making an open and authentic connection with oneself, another person or group of people and then allowing verbal or nonverbal communication to flow through this connection. (Elephant Walk,

Fountain of Love, Group Knot, Group Story, Hand-to-Hand Communication, Human Spring, I Bless You, I Trust You, I Support You, I Imagine, Learning to See Each Other, Meditation Dance, Mirroring, Moving Statues, Planets, Rain, Stand Up, Unfolding).

- *Feedback of Personal Experience.* To process, ground and integrate the entire session for participants.

- *Closing Games.* To complete the session by bringing participants' attention back to the group as a group and to their relationship with it (Group Spiral, I Bless You, I Trust You, I Support You, Meditation Dance, Planets. Note that Appreciation Circles 1-2-3 are only for groups which have been together for a while).

Many games obviously have multiple purposes and values, and thus how many games of each type and which specific games you choose for any given group are left to your intuition and attunement.

It is the author's experience that by including at least *one game of each type in the sequence given above,* the development of trust, openness and cohesiveness will be fostered within any group which is ready and open for the *Playful Self-Discovery* experience. Flexibility and creativity come in selecting the games to use and in tailoring them to the specific group, as well as in the unique style of the facilitator.

A word of caution about choosing games. Decide which games you feel good about leading and which ones you do not. Avoid choosing a game if you have some reservations about it (for example, if you feel it is too long, boring, silly or pointless), although it may be useful personally to examine the nature of your resistance to it. Be assured that *all* of the exercises and games in this book have demonstrated their effectiveness when used at the right time with the right group.

Doing Name Games

Always do a name game of some kind. Even in a small established group, not everyone may know each other's name. If by chance they do, the game will go very quickly, and nothing is lost. Besides, *you* need to know everyone's name so you may use people's names during the session and later. If possible, check a list of participants beforehand to familiarise yourself with any unusual names so that you may use them easily and correctly during the session.

Building Trust One by One

Build trust in the group by including several games which call for participants to work together in pairs, as doing so allows personal one-to-one contact to be made. The important point to remember is that the more *individuals* a person relates to *one at a time* during a session, the more likely that person will be able to be more open and to trust them when they are all together in the group.

Feeding Back Personal Experience

In your planning, allow time for feedback of personal experience from participants, both after each exercise or game and in a special time for feedback near the end of the overall session. Inviting feedback as to how participants have experienced the games is particularly important in the second part of the session when participants' inner responses to the deeper exercises are not as obvious to everyone. Refer to 'Processing the Games' in the following section.

Tailoring Games

Tailor the games to the specific group so that the session is more relevant to participants, and so that you can help them to have a deeper, more meaningful experience. Make it a practice to:

● Use freely whatever jargon is relevant to the group (for example, they may all be doctors, nurses, social workers, teachers, or have similar interests and so on.) Find ways to bring topical words and phrases into your game introductions naturally.

● Choose games which allow you to address group interests. For example, by doing 'Sentence Completion' for a health-related group, you might use such questions as, "I think most doctors are . . . ," "The part of me which needs healing most is . . . ,"

"Sometimes I get sick because I need . . . ," and "My favourite way of getting sick is . . . ."

- Deal directly with group issues or themes. For example, by doing 'Free Association' for a Stress Management group, you might use such triggering sentences as, "Play is . . . ," "Having fun means . . . ," "The way I most like to relax is . . . ," and "What keeps me from playing more in my life is . . ." Thus you plant seeds which can be harvested later.

Using Outlines

Draw up an outline to show the sequence and timing of the games you have chosen to present. (Refer to 'Recommended Session Formats', page 40.) Include an estimated timing column which allows you to monitor your progress throughout the session. Knowing early enough that the session is running considerably later than planned gives you the choice of omitting one or more games as you go along, and thus able to conclude in perhaps a more significant or effective way.

Rehearsing for Clarity and Confidence

Prepare in advance what you plan to say and how you plan to say it. Rehearse *aloud* the directions you plan to give for each game. See how brief you can make them. Avoid taking more time to give instructions than it takes to do the exercise or game!

On the other hand, if you keep getting questions from attentive participants after you give instructions, you are likely being either unclear or incomplete. Beginning facilitators sometimes assume they will be inspired in the moment and will muddle through with the grace of God. As a rule, you will only be as effective as your preparation.

Adding Games to Your Repertoire

When you are practised and confident with the games presented in this book, look for other games to add to your repertoire. Choose games which have an *extra dimension* to them. Make sure they either test trust, give opportunity for people to touch each other physically in non-threatening ways, put them in contact with their feelings, open their hearts, demonstrate important values and principles or fit into other categories of games listed above. Choose games which help you achieve the primary purpose of *Playful Self-Discovery*, that is, to build trust and openness in the group to help it come together as a group.

Collecting Materials and Equipment

Decide which materials (tape playback machine, audio tapes, cushion, ball, blindfolds, post cards and so on) you need for the session and collect them together. It is also a good idea to have boxes of tissues in the room for participants, as exercises and games may sometimes prompt tears of joy or sadness. Also for games which require participants to sit or lie on the floor (such as 'Unfolding'), supplying a blanket for each couple or group helps them to define and stay within their own space, and offers a soft, warm, gentle touch, even if the floor is carpeted.

Making a Final Pre-Session Check

Arrive 10-15 minutes early to the room and check that everything is prepared, including yourself and the following items.

- Ascertain that the room is clean, warm and adequately ventilated, with chairs and other furniture moved out of the room.

- Check the sound system to make sure it is working properly.

- Cue up all audio cassette tapes you plan to use.

- Prepare the room in a short creative visualisation, if you wish, for the activity which is to follow, seeing it clean and pure, warm and supportive, receptive and ready for your group.

- Have lively music playing as participants enter the room.

- Play quieter music as participants return after the refreshment break to help them settle into the gentler atmosphere of the second part.

PRESENTING THE SESSION

For *Playful Self-Discovery*, do see *all* games as having three parts:

- Presenting instructions for the game
- Playing the game
- Processing the game

Consider these parts as legs of a three-legged stool: they all are needed for the stool/game to be of value. Beginning facilitators occasionally are tempted to omit the third part because of time. Doing so is an error in their planning or presenting skills and takes away from their effectiveness. Always save time in every game for all three parts.

PRESENTING INSTRUCTIONS FOR THE GAME

Introduce yourself. Stay light and lively. Model fun, enthusiasm and expectancy. Tell the group what it will be doing. Include these points, using your own language and style:

- Today is a chance for you to relax, have some fun together, get to know yourself and each other better and perhaps begin to relate in new ways.

- The games we will be doing facilitate our coming together as a group. So today allows the blending of unique individuals into a larger whole, in much the same way that individual instruments combine in an orchestra while still maintaining their own distinctive identities.

- Try to stay aware of others in the group, so together we create an atmosphere of openness, safety and support for each other. We all need to stay aware and watch out for each other so that there are no accidents, and so that everyone feels included and has a good time.

- The games are mainly for fun, although many of them can help you to discover more about yourself and can be experienced on several levels. You can choose the level you want to take them on; they can be as deep and challenging or as superficial as you want. For many people, the process is like peeling off the layers of an onion. When you are ready to peel off one layer of awareness, you will find another layer beneath for you to explore.

● There is no right way or wrong way to do any of these games, so just relax into them without worrying about whether you are doing them properly. Also these games have no winners or losers, so no one needs to worry about being the best (or avoiding being the worst) player today. Your only task is to let the 'child within' out to play, so see how spontaneous you can be.

● You may already be familiar with some of these exercises and games. If so, notice how your experience is different today from the last time you played them with a different group of people in a different setting.

● It is perfectly all right to let yourself openly experience anything that occurs to you, laughter, tears, nervousness, embarrassment or other feelings. Often such responses seem magnified in a group because we share them as a group. You will have time to talk about anything you may experience, either in the group or privately if you wish, at the refreshment break or later during the day.

Give all instructions simply, slowly, clearly and loudly. Refer to the examples of instructions given in the 'Exercises and Games' section beginning on page 43.

Explain wherever possible the *purpose* of each game to increase the learning and experiencing potential of each participant and the group as a whole while the process is actually taking place. Decide game by game whether the explanation will have greater effect if it comes before or after playing the game.

If you are working with a co-facilitator, it is essential for the person who starts an exercise or game also to end it to avoid confusion, rather than having it ended by the person who is to introduce the next game.

Be aware of the immediate response the group may have to anything you are explaining, and, if necessary, repeat your instructions (using different words) clearly and simply until you become aware that they understand, or are willing to try the exercise or game anyway, even if they do not completely understand.

The easiest and best way to introduce an exercise or game is to *demonstrate* it *while* giving the instructions, preferably with a co-facilitator. It is especially important for 'eyes-closed' exercises (particularly if a high trust level has not yet been established), as it will be more reassuring to the group if you first explain clearly and demonstrate what is going to take place *before* actually having the group do it.

When using music in exercises or games, be aware of the volume, as it can detract from your effectiveness if it is so loud that it drowns out your voice, calls undue attention to itself or otherwise blasts through an atmosphere you are endeavouring to create. Unless you are using music for a dance, make sure you keep it in the background as a supportive enhancement.

After giving instructions for a game and before you start playing it, always ask participants if they have any questions. Avoid asking, "Does everyone understand?" because some participants may not want to admit they do not understand, but will ask a question if invited. So the recommended approach is to ask, "Are there any questions?"

PLAYING THE GAME

Concentrate on developing a sense of timing so you learn how long to continue a game. It is far better for participants to want more of a game than for them to become bored with it because it has continued too long. Practise feeling the peak of the enthusiasm for a game and moving on to the next game before it fades noticeably.

Most of the time your focus of attention needs to be on the group, observing participants and how they are engaging in the exercises and games. However, it is also usually possible to find a spare moment to check on your next game and materials needed, cue up the next tape you plan to use and check your outline to ascertain how closely you are following your estimated time.

Create a warm atmosphere and a safe environment by being the embodiment of expectant fun yourself. By your example encourage participants to bring out 'the playful child within'. Let your sense of humour show, and let participants see a twinkle in your eyes. Be joyful. It all comes naturally from your enthusiasm. Therefore only agree to facilitate a *Playful Self-Discovery* session when you feel you can be entirely enthusiastic about it. Enthusiasm is contagious.

So is boredom. If after having done several sessions you find yourself becoming bored with certain exercises or games, it may be because you are focusing on the *games* rather than the *people* you are meant to be serving. Focusing on the people will help to revitalise your attention and presence, and consequently your effectiveness as a facilitator. Always keep in mind the larger purpose of the session: you are facilitating a *group process* intended to bring people together. The exercises and games are only the vehicle to take the group to where it needs to go.

By keeping your manner light and lively and by keeping the action always moving forwards, you can deepen the experience for participants without the session becoming overly intense for everyone.

PROCESSING THE GAME

Sometimes the processing or integration takes place spontaneously *during* the game (for example, 'Group Knot'), but usually time needs to be given for it after the game, most especially *after all non-verbal games* (for example, 'Blind Sculptor', 'Elephant Walk', 'Unfolding').

Basically you are doing *Playful Self-Discovery expressly* to help people to open up and talk freely with one another. Therefore avoid subverting this most important process by feeling the pressure of time and hurrying on to the next game in the outline without allowing sufficient time for communication, processing and integration.

As a rule, it is preferable to omit one or more games if necessary because of a shortage of time, rather than to shorten everything and push on relentlessly without regard to the quality of experience you are providing to participants, simply to honour your original plan.

Therefore attune to the group, and allow the discussion after a game to continue until it peaks, and only then conclude it gently.

Participants usually need a sense of completion with each game if they are to be entirely attentive and focused for the next game.

Two words of caution about personal discussion. First, look for ways to vary it with each game so that participants do not find it becoming monotonous, mechanical and forced. Second, monitor closely all after-game talking and move on before it deteriorates into irrelevant chit-chat.

After a Break

Start the second half of the session with a more subdued tone for the quieter part to follow. For example, ask the participants to form a circle, hold hands, close their eyes and listen while you say, "Let us leave the break behind us now and focus our attention on this group once again. Let us bring ourselves fully present into this room, into this group, into this moment. Now, in this second, quieter part, we play games which take us more deeply inside ourselves, and so let us open to the opportunity of learning more about ourselves and each other."

Personal Feedback

Always save time for a specific feedback period towards the end of *Playful Self-Discovery*. It helps ground people's experience and gives them a sense of completion. Encourage them to relate their own experience of the session (for example, which exercises and games most affected them and in which ways), as learning how it has been for each other helps everyone in this process.

• Have the group sit in a circle to focus group attention, provide safety and serve as a relaxed setting for greater openness and trust.

• As much of *Playful Self-Discovery* is directed towards *feeling* rather than *thinking,* people often need time to 'shift gears' and organise their thoughts before describing their experience. So as the facilitator, relax into the pauses which may occur between each person's contribution rather than end the feedback period prematurely.

- While not everyone is expected to speak, time should be given for those participants who wish to do so, however briefly.

- Be aware if participants start to move from a 'feeling' state to a 'mental' state. Throughout the feedback continue to focus on how people *feel*. Avoid analyses and rationalisations as they move the focus from heart to head. Keep bringing participants back to their feelings.

- It is unnecessary for you as facilitator to respond in any way (beyond a sincere 'Thank you for sharing'), or to feel you need to defend, justify or explain anything which happens during a session. If someone offers critical comments, simply receive them as an expression of that person's experience. Such points are valid for the person making them, but they may or may not be useful to you. In either case, by not reacting, you make the climate safe for others in the group to speak out openly.

- If someone is particularly critical, it often helps to ask the others, "How about the rest of you? How do you feel about this point?" By staying out of the discussion yourself, you encourage participants to talk to each other and to resolve or accept differences, thus avoiding polarising debate. It is always useful in such cases to make this 'reality check', that is, to compare your own perceptions of an experience or event with those of other people involved.

- Scheduling the feedback period before the very end of your time together and following it with at least one more game, helps participants remain in a feeling state as they leave the session.

- Essentially your task during the feedback period is simply to give participants the opportunity to draw the threads of their experience together, compare experiences, and complete the session on a warm, positive note.

Later, to help participants stay with their feelings after the entire session is over, sometimes it is useful to conclude by saying, "Before you leave the room, make sure you give at least three people a hug," as it helps participants to ground their feelings, express anything else which may still be present for them and complete their experience of the session.

Participants with Disabilities

Disabled group members should neither be excluded nor allowed to exclude themselves, either by not attending the session at all, or, if attending, by sitting on the sidelines for some (or all) games as passive observers. Sometimes even older, able-bodied participants want to sit out, rest and watch, especially after the first few active games.

While people should not be forced to participate, it is essential, if the group-building purpose of the session is to be achieved, for *everyone* to feel connected with the group throughout the session.

The challenge for the facilitator then is to find creative ways to include *everyone* in *all* exercises and games. For example, if doing a circle dance or game, place the participant who is in a wheelchair in the *centre* of the circle, rather than to one side of it. Then watch the person beam as everyone else dances or plays around him or her!

Once during 'Unfolding', a participant who was unable to move down to the floor and was ready to sit out, was invited simply to remain standing, and to bend over from the waist with arms and hands extended towards the floor. Her partner then proceeded to 'unfold' her into an open, upright position. This variation worked effectively for her and kept her participating fully in the game and in the group.

Over the years, the author has seen many people in wheelchairs participate with the rest of the group in tag and other action games and even 'dance' by moving their chairs rhythmically to the music. Suffice it to say that you may rely on disabled people to find their own ways to adapt if you encourage them to do so. Thus you help them feel included as part of the group, rather than sidelined because of their disability.

Repeat Sessions

The author, while a staff member of the Findhorn Foundation in Scotland, frequently encountered guests who, having travelled from as far away as Australia, had enrolled in four, five or six different week-long residential courses scheduled one after the other. In each course the guests took part in a scheduled session of *Playful Self-Discovery.*

When queried, most guests said how different each session was for them (different exercises and games, different participants, different facilitators and styles; they said even *they* were different from one week to the next), with the result that most guests felt each session had provided a new and deeper experience from which they benefited.

Consequently, it is usually possible, even desirable, for a follow-up *Playful Self-Discovery* session to be presented to the same group. If you decide to facilitate a second session for a group, feel free to include one or more games you led before. The author almost always includes 'Name Chain', 'Hug Tag' and 'Unfolding' in every session he facilitates, simply because he has learned through experience that (like children who never tire of listening to their favourite fairy tales) many adult participants have their favourite games which they like to play over and over again.

Three Primary Tasks

You have three main tasks in facilitating a *Playful Self-Discovery* session:

1. Be authentic. Being yourself makes it safe and gives implicit permission for all participants to be themselves. Remember, the session is not something you do *to* participants, or even *for* them, but rather *with* them. Note, however, that being part of the group means you still hold the focus, direction, and ultimate responsibility for the session.

2. Have the instructions for each game clearly and thoroughly in mind, and present them simply and directly.

3. Guide the flow of the session intuitively, spontaneously and creatively. Stay open and available to the possibility of making changes, and heart connections, in every moment.

All of these principles and techniques may seem quite formidable. However, like learning any skill, all it takes to learn how to facilitate an effective *Playful Self-Discovery* session are the discipline, patience and persistence to become proficient by taking one step at a time.

RECOMMENDED SESSION FORMATS

The following basic *Playful Self-Discovery* formats have been used in the Findhorn Foundation guest programme and education department for many years.

Both are standard four-hour sessions. Note that listing clock times allows you to monitor your progress during the session and make adjustments as necessary. Estimated running times given in parentheses are average times and may vary widely depending upon group size, attention and level of awareness.

It is recommended that you follow the 'Session One' format as closely as possible with three different groups to gain experience in how the session works before you start to adapt it to your own style.

The 'Session One' outline is provided as a guide to beginning facilitators. It is not recommended to be used with any group at any time as a rigid formula. However, it is the author's experience that 'Session One' as presented herein is effective with many groups which are open and ready for the experience.

After facilitating 'Session One' a few times, begin to discover for yourself which games go best with others and which order to present them in to guide the group most effectively to achieve the overall purpose of *Playful Self-Discovery*: helping the group to come together.

When you start to experiment, be sure to strike a balance between light and intense games, active and quiet games, verbal and non-verbal games, and games involving the mind and games involving music and movement.

Sequence them so as to move gently from one type of game to another without 'stripping gears'. The whole session will flow smoothly when you have done your homework properly and when you stay attuned to the group in the moment.

For more information about the process of attunement, refer to 'Inner Problem-Solving', 'Attunement Exercise' and 'Need for Discernment', pages 90-92 in *Bringing More Love Into Your Life: The Choice is Yours,* by Eileen Caddy and David Earl Platts. ISBN 0 905249 75 5.

SESSION ONE

This format was developed by the author in the early 1980s for use in the 'Experience Week', a seven-day residential course at the Findhorn Foundation where, with variation, it continues to be the basic introduction to *Playful Self-Discovery*.

Starting Time	Game	Duration
2.00	Introduction	(5)
2.05	Greeting Dance	(10)
2.15	Name Chain	(10)
2.25	Hug Tag	(10)
2.35	People-to-People	(10)
2.45	Cows and Ducks	(10)
2.55	Group Knot	(15)
3.10	Shoulder Massage	(5)
3.15	Moving Statues	(15)
3.30	Car-Car	(10)
3.40	Lap Sit	(5)
3.45	Group Spiral	(5)
3.50	Refreshment Break	(20)
4.10	Mirroring	(20)
4.30	Hand-to-Hand Communication	(20)
4.50	Unfolding (In Pairs)	(20)
5.10	Feedback of Personal Experience	(15)
5.25	Planets	(20)
5.45	Meditation Dance	(10)
5.55	Completion and Hugs	(5)

SESSION TWO

Once groups have experienced the joy of *Playful Self-Discovery*, they often ask to have follow-up sessions. 'Session Two' is sometimes used by the author as a starting point when preparing for a group which has already participated in a basic 'Session One' presentation.

Starting Time	Game	Duration
2.00	Introduction	(5)
2.05	Name Chain	(10)
2.15	Hug Tag	(10)
2.25	Sentence Completion	(10)
2.35	Humless	(15)
2.50	Energy Creation	(15)
3.05	Human Spring	(5)
3.10	Elephants' Scratch	(5)
3.15	Elephant Walk	(15)
3.30	Blind Sculptor	(15)
3.45	Car Wash	(20)
4.05	Refreshment Break	(20)
4.25	Free Association	(15)
4.40	Nicknames	(10)
4.50	Learning to See Each Other	(10)
5.00	Unfolding (In Groups)	(30)
5.30	Feedback of Personal Experience	(15)
5.45	I Bless You, I Trust You, I Support You	(10)
5.55	Completion and Hugs	(5)

EXERCISES
AND
GAMES

EXERCISES AND GAMES

The exercises and games which follow may be included in either a *Playful Self-Discovery* session or in the 'Preparation Session' which precedes it. Their specific uses are indicated below the title. Refer to *Chart 1, Primary Uses of Exercises and Games,* pages 124-5, for a summary of these uses.

It is recommended that you follow the 'Session One' format (page 41) as closely as possible with three different groups to gain experience in how the session works before you start to adapt it.

Note that these exercises and games are not equally suitable for all groups at all times, so before you begin to choose activities to present, attune to your group to ascertain its special needs. Equally important, also attune to the most appropriate *sequence* of the activities you select to provide maximum effectiveness. Remember, for all groups, trust must be built step by step.

If you are new to leading groups or are not entirely comfortable with leading groups, word-for-word instructions are offered to help you to get started. Eventually, with practice, you will find ways of making the instructions your own, adapting them to your own style and to the group, so that you feel natural and comfortable with all that you say.

Instructions in regular typeface may be said directly to the group. In a few exceptions regular typeface is also used when the entire instructions for an exercise or game are directed solely to the facilitator.

Instructions in italic typeface and enclosed within parentheses are meant for the *Playful Self-Discovery* facilitator only and are not meant to be said to the group.

A final word. Take every opportunity throughout the *Playful Self-Discovery* session to relate the exercises and games to the themes of openness, trust and group consciousness. You thus help participants experience the session within a wider context and on a deeper level of awareness.

Above all, have fun with the games.

ALLY EXERCISE
(Preparing the Group)

Schedule an 'Ally Exercise' as soon as possible (within the first hour) when a new group meets for the first time. Its purpose is to divide the group into pairs to do an exercise, and thus provide each person with an ally, someone to make friendly contact with from the very beginning to help everyone feel more at ease, secure and present.

Playful Self-Discovery is normally scheduled only after a group has been together for a while during which time some form of 'Ally Exercise' will have already been provided. If not, then include an 'Ally Exercise', either as part of a 'Preparation Session' (Refer to 'Preparing the Group', page 20), or if necessary, as part of the *Playful Self-Discovery* session, scheduled prior to the opening game.

An 'Ally Exercise' usually gives participants a task to do. A common task is to introduce themselves to each other (which also prepares them for later 'Personal Introductions'), giving such details as:

1. Their name and where they live
2. An interesting fact or two about themselves, perhaps something about their work, hobby, family and so on
3. Why they have come to the group and what they would like to get from it, that is, their needs and expectations
4. What they are willing to give to the group, such as qualities, skills, time and so forth
5. What fears, questions or concerns they have about the group
6. What they need from the group to feel comfortable being a member of it, such as clarity, confidentiality, honesty, respect and so on

For advanced groups a less structured but more risky variation is simply for partners to begin a series of sentences with the words 'I am . . .', and complete them spontaneously with descriptive statements about themselves.

The 'Ally Exercise' may take many different forms, prompted by whatever the group facilitator may decide is needed in the beginning stages of the group. For another example of an exercise which may be used as an 'Ally Exercise' refer to 'I Imagine', page 91.

ANIMAL IDENTIFICATION
(Exploration Game)

Choose a partner and decide who is 'A' and who is 'B'. Find your own place in the room and sit facing one another. Close your eyes, and take a few deep breaths

(Pause 1 minute, then continue with the following instructions.)

Now from your imagination, allow the name of an animal to come to you, one which you identify closely with in some way, either a wild animal, a domestic animal or a fantasy animal, perhaps a favourite or a very special animal. When you have the name of the animal, open your eyes.

(Pause 1 minute, then continue with the following instructions.)

Now 'A', take three minutes to describe your animal to your partner, *without naming it,* using 'I' statements, as though describing yourself. For example, if your animal is a dog, you might say, "I am dependable and loyal. I have a gentle disposition most of the time, but when my space is invaded, I can become ferocious. I seem to alternate between periods of having great vitality and needing complete rest."

'B', your task is to be a good listener, giving your partner full attention, eye contact and support. *Listen carefully to all your partner tells you.*

Are there any questions? Ready. Begin.

(Pause 3-5 minutes, then continue with the following instructions.)

Change roles. 'B', describe your animal to your partner using 'I' statements, and 'A', *give your partner your full attention.*

Are there any questions? Ready. Begin.

(Pause 3-5 minutes, then continue with the following instructions.)

Now find another couple to form a group of four people.

A psychological principle says you tend to create your own reality with processes known as identification, projection and transference by seeing in your outer environment aspects that you actually carry within yourself. In other words, whatever you *see* is a function of who you *are*, at least in that moment. So whatever qualities and conditions you have just seen and described in your animal are actually aspects of yourself.

Next take one minute to introduce your *partner* to the rest of your group, *describing your partner in human terms* based on the description you have just heard. Using the example above, "David is dependable and loyal. He has a gentle disposition most of the time, but when his space is invaded, he can become ferocious. He seems to alternate between periods of having great vitality and needing complete rest."

(After 4-5 minutes, continue with the following instructions.)

Form a circle. In one sentence, introduce your partner to the whole group, giving his or her name, two or three basic characteristics, and presenting him or her with an imaginary gift, perhaps something which may relate to how he or she has described himself or herself to you.

(When everyone is finished, invite participants to talk about their experience with the exercise.)

(A variation of this game is called 'Object Identification'. *Place on a tray several small everyday objects such as a book, button, calendar, candle, clock, crystal, diary, key, matches, pencil, rubber band, ruler, safety pin, scissors, tape and so on — twice the number of objects as participants — and let the participants select one and proceed throughout the exercise using the object in place of the animal.)*

(Another variation is to have participants go outside, perhaps during an extended refreshment or meal break, and find an object in nature which attracts their attention with which they can identify, such as a flower, feather, leaf, stone, twig and so on. Refer to 'Group Discovery: The Early Days', *pages 11-13, for an illustration of this variation.)*

APPRECIATION CIRCLE 1
(Closing Game)

The 'Appreciation Circle' is used only in groups which have been together long enough for everyone to have had some authentic observation and experience of each other. It is therefore not used in a *Playful Self-Discovery* session within the first few days of newly-formed groups. At the Findhorn Foundation, it is sometimes used on the last afternoon of a seven-day residential course.

The 'Appreciation Circle' sets aside time for each member of a group to receive affirming heart-felt observations from the others. All statements are genuine and sincere and come from personal experience with the person being appreciated. It is not a time to offer criticism, make suggestions or give advice, but rather to recognise, acknowledge, and empower. The person being appreciated accepts the appreciation with a simple 'Thank you,' but says nothing more (or else the appreciation may be deflected, lost or otherwise not taken in fully by the person.)

Group members' observations might include specific ways they have seen the person develop during their time together, admirable qualities and traits they have noticed in the person, laudable accomplishments the person has achieved, contributions he or she has made to the group and other sincere appreciations intended to provide positive reinforcement.

Not everyone needs to say something about everyone else as it is unnecessary to repeat whatever someone else has said. However it is important that the group facilitator says something to everyone. The 'Appreciation Circle' may either be planned or may be spontaneous. Here is an example of each.

1. An ongoing, open-ended group may periodically set aside time for everyone to be appreciated. Meetings may start or end with an 'Appreciation Circle' where everyone is the subject of appreciation for 1-5 minutes, depending on the size of the group and the time available.

2. *Any* group may have an 'Appreciation Circle' at *any* time. The author was once the guest of honour at a surprise birthday party where an impromptu 'Appreciation Circle' took place for him.

APPRECIATION CIRCLE 2
(Closing Game)

For this exercise, a ball of woollen yarn is required.

Refer to 'Appreciation Circle 1' for background information about this exercise.

The group sits quite closely to each other on the floor in a circle. Each participant has the opportunity to appreciate another, that is, to express sincere observations and perceptions of the person to provide positive reinforcement, encouragement and support.

The facilitator firmly holds the end of the yarn in one hand while holding the ball of yarn in the other. The facilitator selects a person to appreciate and throws the ball of yarn to that person who catches it and then listens to the facilitator's appreciations of one or two sentences. For example, "I appreciate the way you listen to others and give them your full attention." Or, "I appreciate your sense of humour and how you use it to help people feel at ease." Or, "I appreciate the risks you have taken in the group by being very honest and open about yourself."

The person who has been appreciated then continues the process by holding onto the strand of yarn in one hand and throwing the ball of yarn to another person in the circle who catches it and then listens to the next appreciation.

The procedure continues until everyone has been appreciated, and depending upon the size of the group, the ball of yarn has been used up.

Then, while the participants continue to hold onto their strand of yarn, the facilitator points out the web of interconnections *formed by their expression of appreciation, acceptance and respect for each other.*

The facilitator may then ask the participants to close their eyes and visualise the web of interconnections taking place also on the inner planes of body, mind and Spirit.

APPRECIATION CIRCLE 3
(Closing Game)

Refer to 'Appreciation Circle 1' for background information about this exercise.

On the final day of courses which run several days, or in ongoing groups which come to an end, all participants are given time to say or do whatever they wish *to complete their experience of the course or group,* perhaps indicating major experiences or learnings, significant interactions, high points, low points, meaningful accomplishments and so on.

They may have something they need to say to one person in the group or to the whole group. They may wish to give a gift to the group, such as to recite a poem, sing a song or perform a dance. It is their time to use as they choose in order to feel complete, after which they are appreciated by the rest of the group for the time they have remaining.

For example, if three hours are set aside for this completion process, and 20 people are in the group, each person has nine minutes of group time. If an individual does not take all nine minutes in personal sharing, the remainder of the time is given over to the other participants appreciating that person.

It is each person's responsibility to decide how to use the allotted time.

BLIND SCULPTOR
(Trust and Close-Touching Game)

Find two partners and decide who is 'A', 'B', and 'C'. This game, 'Blind Sculptor', tests your attunement, trust and spatial memory. It is a non-verbal exercise, so remain silent for the entire exercise. You will have time to talk about your experience with it later.

A blind sculptor has been commissioned to replicate a famous statue. 'A' is the first sculptor, 'B' is the first model and 'C' is the first clay. The sculptor and the clay keep their eyes closed throughout the game. As the model, 'B', you place yourself in any classic pose to become the original statue. As the clay, 'C', you make yourself available for the sculptor to use to replicate the pose.

Since the sculptor is blind, 'A', you first have to approach the statue, use your hands to get a sense of the pose and then you move to the clay and position it in the same pose. Working steadily, take no more than two or three minutes to complete the statue. When you are finished, the sculptor says, "Ready," and both of you then open your eyes and appreciate how well the sculptor has managed to replicate the original statue.

After the first statue is finished, change roles, with 'B' the sculptor, 'C' the model and 'A' the clay. And then later change again so that each of you plays all three roles. When a group completes all three statues, remain silent and enjoy the other groups finishing their statues. Are there any questions? Ready. Begin.

(When everyone is finished, continue with the following instructions.)

Now take a few minutes to talk in your groups about your experience in each one of the three roles: sculptor, statue and clay. Which one was the easiest role? Which one was the most challenging?

CAMERA WALK
(Trust and Exploration Game)

Choose a partner, decide who is 'A and 'B' and stand together. This exercise helps you to experience seeing from another person's perspective. It is a non-verbal exercise, so remain silent for the entire exercise. You will have time to talk about your experience with it later.

'A', you close your eyes and allow 'B' to lead you about the room in search of interesting photographs to take. 'B' becomes the camera viewfinder for 'A' by leading 'A' to an interesting object, setting, person or whatever you wish 'A' to experience. You may need to position 'A's body and head to achieve the required angle and distance for the desired photo composition.

'B', you form your hands into a rectangle in front of 'A's eyes (simulating the camera viewfinder), and when you are ready, you give a signal to 'A' to open your eyes (the camera shutter), until 'B' gives a signal to 'A' to close your eyes again. You can vary the length of time you have your partner keep his or her eyes open, and you can move as slowly or as quickly around the room as you wish taking pictures. After a few minutes I will stop you, and then you will reverse roles. Are there any questions? Ready. Begin.

(Pause 5-10 minutes, then continue with the following instructions.)

Stop! Everyone stop. Now reverse roles, with 'B' closing your eyes and 'A' taking the pictures.

(Pause 5-10 minutes, then conclude by inviting the participants to talk about their experience, either with their partner or in the group.)

(If time and the floor plan allow, a variation is to let participants leave the room and explore other parts of the building, but for safety's sake only if no stairs have to be used. Another variation, if the weather and environs allow, is to let participants go outside into the surrounding landscape. With either of these variations, allow from 10-20 minutes per person. 'B' is told to watch the time and to reverse roles when half the time is left. After the second round, everyone returns to the room to process and conclude the exercise.)

CAR-CAR
(Trust and Close-Touching Game)

(Suggestion. Use this game with groups doing Playful Self-Discovery *for the first time. Use* 'Elephant Walk', *page 65 with groups which have already experienced this game.)*

Choose a partner, decide who is 'A' and who is 'B' and stand together. This game is called 'Car-Car', and it helps you experience how you feel about trust. It is a non-verbal exercise, so remain silent for the entire exercise. You will have time to talk about your experience with it later.

'A' is the car first, so you put your hands up in front of your chest, palms outward, to serve as your bumpers. If you feel more daring during the game, you may later drop your arms to your sides. 'B' is the driver first, so you stand behind 'A' and put your hands on your partner's shoulders.

'A', close your eyes and 'B', *keeping your eyes open,* you guide 'A' around the room, steering with your hands and turning 'A' about to avoid collisions with other cars. 'A', try not to open your eyes. Do not judge yourself if you do, but be aware that it is what you have had to do to feel safe.

'A', notice your feelings during this game. How trusting are you? Do you hesitate, or do you give control over easily to someone else? 'B', notice how you feel about being trusted to be totally responsible and to exercise caution, knowing someone else is depending completely upon you to keep him or her safe. After a few minutes I will stop you, and then you will reverse roles. Are there any questions? Ready. Begin.

(After 2-3 minutes, continue with the following instructions.)

Stop! Everyone stop. Without talking, 'B', close your eyes and put your hands up in front of your chest. 'A', keeping your eyes open, begin to guide your partner about in perfect safety and trust.

(After 2-3 minutes, continue with the following instructions.)

Stop! Everyone stop. Now take a few minutes to talk about your experience with each other in both roles as the car and as the driver.

CAR WASH
(Trust and Close-Touching Game)

(This game is more comfortable played on a carpeted floor. If you have to use a room with a wood, tile or composition floor, provide cushions for people to use. If you have more than 24 participants, divide the group into two halves and have two separate car washes. A variation is to do this game with all participants standing.)

(It can be fascinating and revealing for the facilitator to observe how, using the metaphor of the car for oneself, people unconsciously tend to describe themselves and their own needs as they describe their cars — also whether they take 5 luxurious minutes or 10 frantic seconds to move through the car wash receiving the full attention of the group.)

Form two lines facing each other, standing closely shoulder to shoulder. The lines should be an arm's length apart. Now kneel down on your hands and knees or sit. You have formed a human 'Car Wash', which is the name of this game. The person at one end moves in between the lines, faces the group and announces what kind of car you are, the condition you are in, and the treatment you need. For example, "I am a brand new, sleek white Corvette and all I need is a gentle polishing," or "I am an old rusty VW which has been sadly neglected for too many years, and I need a good cleaning inside and out."

Then becoming the car, the person crawls slowly down between the lines on hands and knees. The others simulate an automatic car wash and clean, scrub, pat, and polish you, either gently or vigorously, depending on what you say you need, while radiating loving, caring attention to you. Once through the car wash, the person joins the other end of one of the lines, and the next person begins. Are there any questions? Ready. Begin.

(As the game progresses, and the lines build up on one end, you may need to ask the whole group to get up occasionally and move towards the opposite end of the room.)

(When everyone is finished, invite participants to talk about their experience with the exercise.)

CATERPILLAR
(Silly and Close-Touching Game)

Lie down on your stomach as closely together as possible, all facing the same direction, with your arms at your side.

The person on one end begins to roll over onto the next person and keeps rolling over the entire group of people. When you get to the end, take your place lying on your stomach, and the next person at the other end starts rolling over the group, until everyone has had a turn at being a 'Caterpillar', which is the name of this game.

Are there any questions? Ready. Begin.

(As the game progresses and the group builds up on one end, you may need to ask everyone to get up occasionally and move towards the opposite end of the room.)

(When everyone is finished, invite participants to talk about their experience with the exercise.)

CHOOSING A LEADER
(Creative and Exploration Game)

Divide into groups of 6-8 people, and sit in a circle with your group.

Your task is to choose a leader to be responsible for your group. First take a moment to decide within yourself the qualities you value and want in the person chosen to lead your group.

(Pause 1 minute, and then continue with the following instructions.)

Look around your group and explore the faces of the people you see as you search for the qualities you seek in a leader.

(Pause 1 minute, and then continue with the following instructions.)

It is a non-verbal exercise, so remain silent for the entire exercise. You will have time to talk about your experience with it later. So without talking or writing, begin the process of choosing your leader. You may use facial and body gestures, but no words or sounds to make your selection. You need to find someone who is willing to serve as leader, and your group's decision must be unanimous. You have up to 10 minutes, so take your time and select absolutely the very best person to be leader of your group. When you have chosen someone who definitely agrees to be your leader, remain silent and await further instructions after all groups are finished. Are there any questions? Ready. Begin.

(Pause 8-10 minutes or whatever time is needed for all groups to choose a leader, then continue with the following instructions.)

Now take a few minutes to talk about your experience of how your group chose its leader. Examine especially the process of how your leader was chosen. What was the sequence of events which led to the final choice? Who took the most active part? The *actual* leader may not be the one chosen as leader. The one who was the most influential in the process of choosing is in fact the one who led!

(When everyone is finished, invite participants to talk about their experience with the exercise.)

CIRCLE PASS
(Silly Game)

Form a circle and all join hands for a game called 'Circle Pass'.

In this game a pulse of loving energy is sent around the group starting by my squeezing hands with the person on my right who then passes the squeeze on to the next person, and so on and on around the circle until it comes back to me when I will either pass it on again or change it in some way. Let's find out how fast we can go. Are there any questions? Ready. Begin.

(Pause 1-2 minutes, then continue with the following instructions.)

Next we pass the energy squeeze back in the opposite direction by my squeezing hands with the person on my left. Let's try doing it this time with our eyes closed.

(Pause 1-2 minutes, then continue with the following instructions.)

Now let's pass the energy squeeze around the circle in *both* directions starting by my squeezing hands with the people on either side of me.

(Conclude by inviting participants to talk about their experience with the game.)

(A variation of— or addition to— this game passes nonsense syllables or sounds, such as 'Ooh' or 'Aah', around the circle in one or both directions.)

(Another variation passes the word 'Zoom' around the circle as quickly as possible in either direction. Brakes may be added by a person saying 'E-e-e-e-k', with the result that the 'Zoom' reverses directions.)

(Still another variation is one in which a person creates an amusing facial expression, then turns and shows it to the next person who then imitates or mirrors the expression before changing it into a new funny face to pass on to the following person, and so on around the circle.)

COWS AND DUCKS
(Silly and Trust Game)

(This game divides the group into sub-groups which can then be used for a succeeding game, such as 'Moving Statues'.)

Stand in a circle as large as the room permits.

To start our next game, I am going around the circle to whisper in your ear the name of an animal. Talk among yourselves so that you do not hear the names I whisper to the others.

(Go quickly around the circle, whispering the name of one animal for every 6-8 people in the group. Alternate them (for example, cats, cows, ducks, cats, cows, ducks, cats, cows, ducks), so that each resultant sub-group will be more or less the same size. Then continue with the following instructions.)

The object of this game is to find and get together with the rest of the members of your animal family. With your eyes closed, move throughout the room while making the sound of the animal you are supposed to be. When you meet someone from your own animal family, put an arm around the person and together continue moving about the room as a group searching for and gathering up all the others. If you have to open your eyes, it will spoil it for you, as this game is one of trust as well.

This game demonstrates that as individuals you must sound your own distinctive note in the world, in effect saying, 'This is who I am.' Yet at the same time you must listen for other similar notes so that you can form your own affinity and support groups.

I will keep my eyes open, and when I see that you are all clustered in your animal families, I will tell you to stop and open your eyes.

Are there any questions? Ready. Begin.

(When everyone is finished, invite participants to talk about their experience with the exercise.)

CRADLE ROCK
(Trust and Close-Touching Game)

(This game is good to use when one or more group members feel 'unsupported' by the group. Have groups of at least eight participants to give secure support to the person in question. Ensure that one person supports the person's neck and head, with at least three strong people supporting the chest, belly and hips on either side.)

Divide into groups of 8-10 people.

Everyone takes turns while one person at a time lies stretched out on the floor with eyes closed, arms crossed over your chest and hands on your shoulders. The other participants kneel on either side of you and extend their hands and arms underneath you, while one person supports your neck and head. Radiating love, they slowly stand and gently lift you, rocking you back and forth until they raise you to their waist height. The group may hum a lullaby softly if it wishes.

After continuing to rock you back and forth for a few moments, they lower you slowly in the same way, gently returning you to the floor.

Called 'Cradle Rock' this is a trust game, and is one in which you may relax and open yourself to the love and support of the group.

Are there any questions? Ready. Begin.

(When everyone is finished, invite participants to talk about their experience with the exercise.)

CREATING YOUR OWN REALITY
(Exploration Game)

Choose a partner and sit facing each other far enough apart so that you do not touch each other. Look directly and comfortably into each other's eyes, but without staring. It is a non-verbal psychosynthesis exercise, so remain silent throughout it. You will have time to talk about your experience with it later.

Everyone has beliefs, and while you accept your beliefs as being true for you, they may not be true for anyone else. Ken Keyes Jr. says, "A loving person lives in a loving world. A hostile person lives in a hostile world. Everyone you meet is your mirror." If we all live in the *same* world, how can that be?

It is because your beliefs are like tinted sunglasses through which you see the world; and the world, as a mirror, reflects back to you whatever belief you present to it. The kind of world you create and experience for yourself depends upon which glasses you wear, that is, it depends upon your beliefs, even though you may tell yourself it is the other way around. Rue Wallace Hass sums it up clearly and concisely: 'What you see is who you are.' So what do you see? And who then are you? It all depends upon the glasses you wear. It all depends upon your beliefs.

This theory explains how you end up 'Creating Your Own Reality', and this exercise demonstrates it. For you to benefit fully from the exercise, you must be willing to take on a belief about your partner and believe it completely and sincerely for two minutes, not to *pretend* to believe it, not to act *as if* you believe it, but to *actually* believe it about your partner. Are you willing to do it? It is an awareness exercise, so as you maintain eye contact with your partner and believe the belief for two minutes, stay aware of how you react inside yourself to the belief. Are there any questions? Ready. Begin.

Here is the first belief . . . 'This person likes me' . . . 'This person likes me'. . . What happens inside yourself as you hear this belief about your partner? . . . How do you respond physically to this belief? . . . What sensations do you experience? . . . How do you respond emotionally to this belief? . . . What feelings do you experience? . . . How do you respond intellectually to this belief? . . . What thoughts or ideas do you experience? . . . Do you find it easy to believe this belief, or do you distance yourself from it in some way? . . . Whatever your reactions, do not judge yourself . . . But stay aware of your inner responses to this belief about your partner . . . 'This person likes me' . . .

(Pause 1-2 minutes, then continue with the following instructions.)

Now you may take off those glasses . . . Here is a second belief to believe about your partner, a second pair of glasses . . . Continue to make eye contact with your partner . . . 'This person could be a problem for me, this person could hurt me in some way' . . . 'This person could be a problem for me, this person could hurt me in some way' . . .

What happens inside yourself as you hear this belief about your partner? . . . How do you respond physically to this belief? . . . How do you respond emotionally? . . . How do you respond intellectually? . . . Do you find it easy to believe this belief, or do you distance yourself from it in some way? . . . Whatever your reactions, do not judge yourself . . . But stay aware of your inner responses to this belief about your partner . . . 'This person could be a problem for me, this person could hurt me in some way' . . .

(Pause 1-2 minutes, then continue with the following instructions.)

Now you may take off those glasses . . . If you are willing here is a third belief to believe about your partner for two minutes, a third pair of glasses . . . Continue to make eye contact with your partner . . . 'This person has something wonderful to teach me' . . . 'This person has something wonderful to teach me' . . .

What happens inside yourself as you hear this belief about your partner? . . . What sensations do you experience? . . . What feelings do you experience? . . . What thoughts or ideas do you experience? . . . Do you find it easy to believe this belief, or do you distance yourself from it in some way? . . . Whatever your reactions, do not judge yourself . . . But stay aware of your inner responses to this belief about your partner . . . 'This person has something wonderful to teach me' . . .

(Pause 1-2 minutes, then continue with the following instructions.)

Now you may take off those glasses . . . If you are willing here is one last belief to believe about your partner, one last pair of glasses . . . Continue to make eye contact . . . 'This person is a divine being, a soul . . . Infinite . . . Eternal . . . Loving and lovable . . . Perfect just as he or she is' . . . 'This person is a divine being, a soul . . . Infinite . . . Eternal . . . Loving and lovable . . . Perfect just as he or she is' . . .

What happens inside as you hear this belief about your partner? . . . What sensations do you experience? . . . What feelings? . . . What thoughts or ideas? . . . Do you find it easy to believe this belief, or do you distance yourself from it in some way? . . . Whatever your reactions, do not judge yourself . . . But stay aware of your inner responses to this belief about your partner . . . 'This person is a divine being, a soul . . . Infinite . . . Eternal . . . Loving and lovable . . . Perfect just as he or she is' . . .

(Pause 1-2 minutes, then continue with the following instructions.)

Now you may take off those glasses . . . Take a few minutes to talk with your partner about your various responses to each of the four beliefs. Here they are again: 'This person likes me. This person could be a problem to me, this person could hurt me in some way. This person has something wonderful to teach me. This person is a divine being, a soul. Infinite. Eternal. Loving and lovable. Perfect just as he or she is'.

(Afterward in the large group, invite feedback from the participants about their experience with the exercise. Later, make the following points.)

As you all have had different responses with each belief, and as you have had the same partner each time, the reality you created each time was a function of your belief and your inner response to it on all levels. Thus you projected all of your inner responses onto the neutral screen of your partner. How often do we all project onto others in our everyday world? When are we ever *not* wearing the glasses of our beliefs? How often do we ever truly see people as they are?

CUP MASSAGE
(Trust and Close-Touching Game)

Choose a partner, decide who is 'A' and 'B' and stand together.

'A', you keep your hands down at your sides, close your eyes and relax.

'B', you cup each of your hands (as if to carry water in them), and then begin to give your partner a gentle 'Cup Massage', starting with the shoulders and gradually working down the arms, back, bottom and legs. And then go slowly back up your partner's body again.

(Pause 2-3 minutes, then continue with the following instructions.)

Slowly bring your massage to an end. *(Pause.)*

Now reverse roles. 'B', keep your hands down at your sides, close your eyes and relax. 'A', begin to give your partner a gentle 'Cup Massage'.

(Pause 2-3 minutes, then continue with the following instructions.)

Now slowly bring your massage to an end. *(Pause.)*

Next face each other for the final part of the exercise which is to give each other a 'Cup Massage' at the same time!

(Pause 1-2 minutes, then conclude by inviting participants to talk about their experience with the exercise.)

ELEPHANTS' SCRATCH
(Silly and Close-Touching Game)

(This game is good for lifting the energy level of a group. Keep it a gentle, sensual experience rather than a boisterous, athletic one.)

Choose a partner and stand back-to-back for 'Elephants' Scratch'. It is a non-verbal exercise, so remain silent for the entire exercise. You will have time to talk about your experience with it later.

Elephants because of their size have only two ways of scratching themselves: they either find a tree to lean up against, or they find another elephant to lean up against and they scratch each other, a clear example of symbiosis in the wild.

Your task now is to become an elephant scratching yourself by scratching another elephant. With your backs together, keeping your arms and hands down at your sides throughout this exercise, begin to lean against each other, slowly moving up and down, scratching or massaging each other gently with your body.

(Pause 1-2 minutes, then continue with the following instructions.)

Begin to move around your partner so that you scratch or massage each other gently all over with your body. At times you both may be standing side to side, back to front or front to front. Close your eyes, if you wish, relax and enjoy the pure pleasure of the experience.

(Pause 1-2 minutes, then continue with the following instructions.)

Next find another pair of elephants, and the four of you continue to scratch yourselves by scratching each other gently, arms still down at your sides.

(Pause 1-2 minutes, then continue with the following instructions.)

Now find another group of four elephants and the eight of you continue to scratch each other gently.

(Pause 1-2 minutes, then continue with the following instructions.)

As you know, elephants live together in families or herds, so now to finish, all elephants come together and scratch each other gently.

ELEPHANT WALK
(Trust and Attunement Game)

Choose a partner, decide who is 'A' and who is 'B' and stand together. It is a non-verbal exercise, so remain silent for the entire exercise. You will have time to talk about your experience with it later.

This game, called 'Elephant Walk', shows how you feel about trusting others by handing over control to them. 'A' is the elephant first, so you extend your dominant hand in front of you parallel with the floor, as if it were an elephant's trunk. As the trainer, 'B', you put your opposite hand directly under it, so, for example, the palm of 'A's right hand rests lightly on the back of 'B's left hand. 'A', close your eyes. 'B', keep your eyes open, and, side by side, you gently lead 'A' around the room, walking forwards, in circles, backwards and so on.

After a few moments, as you both feel more comfortable, begin to let your hands slide away from each other, so that eventually only one finger of each hand remains in contact, and you communicate by subtle attunement to one another. Monitor your own feelings to learn how it feels to trust someone and to be trusted in this way. After two or three minutes, I will stop you and you will reverse roles.

Are there any questions? Ready. Begin.

(Pause 2-3 minutes, then continue with the following instructions.)

Stop! Everyone stop. Now 'B', you extend your dominant hand and then close your eyes. 'A', you put your opposite hand under 'B's' hand, and keeping your eyes open, gently lead your partner about in perfect safety and trust.

(Pause 2-3 minutes, then continue with the following instructions.)

Stop! Everyone stop.

Now take a few minutes to talk about your experience with each other in both roles as the elephant and as the trainer.

ENERGY CREATION
(Silly and Creative Game)

(With groups of more than 10-12 participants, you may wish to do this game sitting.)

Stand in a circle for 'Energy Creation', an opportunity for you to express your originality and creativity. It is a non-verbal exercise, so remain silent for the entire exercise. You will have time to talk about your experience with it later.

The first person, in mime, using only hand and body gestures silently creates an imaginary object (such as making a kite and then flying it, moulding a typewriter and then typing on it or cooking food and then eating it), and then passes it on to the next person who then reshapes and transforms it into an entirely new object before passing it on to the following person. Take no more than a minute to create your object.

Are there any questions? Ready. Begin.

(When everyone is finished, invite participants to talk about their experience with the exercise.)

EVERYBODY IS IT
(Action and Silly Game)

(This game goes so fast that it is often good fun to repeat it once or twice.)

This tag game is one in which 'Everybody Is It,' and runs around tagging one another. When you are first tagged, hold the place on your body where you are tagged with one hand, and keep moving about tagging others. The second time you are tagged, do the same with your other hand and keep moving. The third time you are tagged, you must freeze in place. The game stops when only one person able to move remains.

Are there any questions? Ready. Begin.

(When everyone is finished, invite participants to talk about their experience with the exercise.)

EVOCATION OF OPENNESS*
(Creative and Exploration Game)

Find your own place in the room and sit or lie quietly. Breathe deeply and relax.

This psychosynthesis exercise presents a method to evoke or manifest a desired quality in your life, today using the quality of Openness. If for physical reasons you are unable to participate fully in this exercise, simply hint or suggest as much as you can with your body. Or, if absolutely necessary, close your eyes and visualise or imagine it all happening.

First, for contrast, allow your body to express or dramatise the quality of *'closedness'*, the opposite of openness . . . Place your body in a highly uncomfortable posture, all knotted up, covering up or burying your head as if hiding away, with your arms and legs askew, shielding your body . . . Exaggerate it as much as you can to help you to get the feel of it in your body . . .

Now close your eyes . . . Feel the actual physical tension and stress you are placing upon your body as you hold this closed position for another moment . . . Notice how much effort and energy it takes . . . Notice how it feels emotionally to be closed down in such a way . . .

(Pause 1 minute, then continue with the following instructions.)

Now relax . . . Feel the difference . . . Feel the contrast . . . Feel the relief . . .

Next open your eyes and allow your body to express or dramatise the quality of *openness,* the opposite of whatever you have been doing . . . From the art and science of Body Language, you may know it means *not* to cross your arms or legs, but rather to maintain a totally free, natural, unguarded position . . . Take on whatever seem to be the most appropriate physical characteristics of openness . . .

Experiment with various body positions, postures, movements and gestures . . . Exaggerate everything you do . . . Make it all real, alive and fun . . . For example, you may wish to express openness on your face with a smile and any other facial gestures which are meaningful to you . . . Allow yourself to be as spontaneous, intuitive and creative as you can be . . .

(Pause 1-2 minutes, then continue with the following instructions.)

Keeping your eyes closed, feel the relaxation (the absence of tension) in your body . . . Feel the freedom . . . Notice how much less effort and energy it takes to be open . . . Notice how it feels emotionally to be open . . . Then begin moving your entire body freely and rhythmically . . . Until at last you find yourself dancing openly . . .

(Pause 1-2 minutes, then continue with the following instructions.)

Once you are satisfied that your body is comfortably expressing openness, turn your attention to your thoughts . . . While continuing to move, begin to think about openness, and all it means to you . . . Reflect upon its benefits and blessings . . . Consider its value and usefulness . . . Appreciate and praise it . . . Realise how positive you are feeling about it . . . Desire it . . . Yearn for it . . . Feel how receptive you are to it . . . Choose to welcome it more and more into your life . . .

(Pause 1-2 minutes, then continue with the following instructions.)

Then begin to evoke openness more directly while continuing to move about the room openly . . . Affirm it aloud . . . Repeat over and over again, "I always feel safe and at ease to be completely open" . . . Feel the truth of the statement . . . Feel the safety . . . Feel the ease . . . Feel the openness . . . Accept it is so . . . Express your openness to everyone else in the room as you continue to move about the room . . .

(Pause 1-2 minutes, then continue with the following instructions.)

Now imagine situations or circumstances which normally would cause you to protect yourself by holding back, distancing yourself or closing down . . . For example, imagine being confronted by a difficult person . . . A difficult problem . . . Other anxious, insecure moments . . . Then *see, feel and sense* yourself to be entirely open and safe . . . Experience your own increased openness . . . Acknowledge it . . . Accept it . . . Appreciate it . . .

(Pause 1-2 minutes, then continue with the following instructions.)

Lastly, commit yourself to remaining as open as you are now throughout the rest of today, no matter what happens . . . Model openness for others . . . Be a living example of it . . . Radiate openness to everyone you meet . . .

(Pause 1-2 minutes, then continue with the following instructions.)

Now choose a partner, and take a few minutes to talk about your experience with the exercise.

*From *Bringing More Love Into Your Life: The Choice Is Yours,* by Eileen Caddy and David Earl Platts, Ph.D. ISBN 0-905249-75-5

EXPECTATIONS
(Preparing the Group)

(Everyone needs pen and paper for this exercise.)

Participants in both new and established groups usually have quite reasonable expectations about what they might give to and receive from the group during their time together. They usually also have idealised hopes, fantasising the very best which could happen, as well as fears, imagining the very worst. It helps to make all of them explicit.

One way of making your *hopes* clear is to complete this sentence in as many ways as you wish, "I will be very disappointed, if by the end of this group *(or by the end of the day, week, month, year, etc.)* . . ."

(Pause 1-2 minutes, then continue with the following instructions.)

To find whatever *fears* you may have about the group, complete this sentence in as many ways as you wish: "I will be very relieved, if by the end of this group (or by the end of the day, week, month, year, etc.) . . ."

(Pause 1-2 minutes, then continue with the following instructions.)

Now each person read out your hopes to the group.

(Pause to allow everyone to do so, then continue with the following instruction.)

Now read out your fears to the group.

(When everyone has finished, make the following point.)

Having positive expectations (or hopes) or negative ones (or fears) limits seriously your potential, both for getting whatever you want from the group, and also for avoiding whatever you do not want from it. Paradoxically, you must release all of your expectations so that you are open to receive whatever you do want. Otherwise, if you hold on to your expectations tightly, then you are not free to accept the real gifts that being in the group has for you, whatever they may be.

(Invite participants to talk about their experience with this exercise.)

EYE CONTACT
(Exploration Game)

This game is called 'Eye Contact'. It is a non-verbal exercise, so remain silent for the entire exercise. You will have time to talk about your experience with it later.

First walk slowly around the room with eyes open, but without making eye contact with anyone else, and become aware of how it feels to you.

(Pause 1-2 minutes, then continue with the following instructions.)

Next, as you walk around the room, begin to make brief eye contact with each other, and become aware of any difference in how the experience feels to you now.

(Pause 1-2 minutes, then continue with the following instructions.)

Now as you walk around the room, make eye contact for a longer time with each other, and begin to communicate silently with each other. Become aware of any difference in how the experience feels to you now.

(Pause 1-2 minutes, then conclude by inviting participants to talk about their experience with the exercise.)

(A variation is to divide into groups of 8-10 people. Each group sits in a circle. Participants are told to make contact and communicate only through their eyes with as many people — one at a time — as they wish for 8-10 minutes.)

FAIRIES AND DRAGONS*
(Silly and Exploration Game)

(This psychosynthesis game demonstrates that you can use your will to choose your behaviour rather than be a victim of it. It is good for lifting the energy level of a group. It also may be used in preparation for a therapeutic session where participants are likely to or intended to cathart.)

Everyone stand and divide into two equal groups.

The first half of the group are fairies, the essence of gentleness, love and joy. You are very lighthearted, dancing about, spreading your fairy dust of good cheer upon everyone you meet, making appropriate sounds, perhaps even singing gaily. Exaggerate it as much as you can.

You know that 'love conquers all', so it actually does not matter if you meet someone else who does not share your mood. Your task is simply to express pure unconditional love out into the world and to take no notice of whatever response you may receive. You may do anything you wish to express your great love for all those you meet, *except you are not allowed to touch anyone in any way.*

The second half of the group are very unfriendly dragons, the essence of anger and power. You are very aggressive, defending your territory from all intruders, especially the fairies. Your task is to intimidate everyone you meet, making loud and angry noises, and demonstrating your power. Exaggerate it as much as you can.

You know that 'might makes right', so impress everyone with your commanding physical strength and domineering ways. Don't forget the fire and smoke blazing from your nostrils and mouth! Be as forceful and as frightening as you can be. You may do anything you wish to express your great anger and power, *except you are not allowed to touch anyone in any way.*

After a few minutes, I will say 'Stop', so do listen for my voice.

Are there any questions? Ready. Begin.

(Pause 2-3 minutes, then continue with the following instructions.)

Stop! Everyone stop. In the next part of this game, everyone reverse roles. The people who were fairies now become dragons.

The people who were dragons now become fairies. Again, after a few minutes I will say 'Stop', so do listen for my voice. Ready. Begin.

(Pause 2-3 minutes, then continue with the following instructions.)

Stop! Everyone stop. In the final part of this game, begin by being either a fairy or a dragon and continue for as long as you wish. Then choose deliberately to become the other role, and carry on for as long as you wish. Then choose deliberately to become the first one again. Continue to alternate between the two roles as often as you like by making deliberate choices.

(Pause 2-3 minutes, then continue with the following instructions.)

Stop! Everyone stop.

(Invite participants to talk about their experience with the exercise, later making the following point.)

One purpose of this game is to demonstrate that you can make deliberate choices about how and when you express your emotions, such as love and anger. It means therefore that you have both the power and the responsibility to decide how and when to express your feelings.

*Adapted from an original exercise created by Judith Firman.

FOUNTAIN OF LOVE
(Exploration and Attunement Game)

Find your own place in the room and sit quietly . . . Close your eyes, take a few deep breaths, and become still . . . Relax your body and let go for the moment of any thoughts, feelings or concerns you may have . . . Breathe out tension . . . Breathe in peace . . .

Now from your imagination allow to come to you an image or sense of a fountain in the centre of the room . . . Notice it is not a water fountain . . . Rather, it is a fountain of love . . . Begin to feel its joy and its purity . . . Its nourishing and healing powers . . . Its inspiration and upliftment . . . Notice the sounds it makes . . .

Now see the waves of this fountain of love flow outward from the centre to every person in the room, bathing everyone in love's wonder and nourishment . . . Feel refreshed and reborn by it . . . Allow this pure love to fill your entire being until you become one with it . . . Feel joy and peace . . . Feel radiant with love, the divine essence within yourself and all people everywhere . . .

Now see this love radiate outward from your heart, flowing into the entire community, uplifting and inspiring everyone it touches, uniting everyone, bringing deep peace and joy . . . See it flow out into the countryside in all directions, touching and filling all people everywhere, until it covers the entire planet . . . See the Earth radiant with love . . .

(Pause 1-2 minutes, then continue with the following instructions.)

In your own time, open your eyes, and as you do, bring the love you are feeling now with you . . . Bring it out . . . Externalise it . . . Continue to experience it fully . . . Accept it as an expression of who you are at the very core of your being, and of who everyone else is as well . . . Look around and make eye contact with others in the room . . . Now begin to walk around the room, and *with your eyes alone,* express your love to the people you meet and receive love from them as well . . .

Now choose a partner and take a few minutes to talk about your experience with the exercise.

FREE ASSOCIATION
(Exploration Game)

(Decide which topic(s) to use with this exercise, tailored to the group, its purpose and needs. Choose one or more topics for participants to explore, such as Commitment, Health, Life, Love, Money, Play, Power, Responsibility, Sex, Trust, Work and so on. It is also a trust game to the extent that participants are willing to speak spontaneously without censoring whatever occurs to them to say.)

Choose a partner and decide who is 'A' and who is 'B'. Sit quietly facing each other and hold hands.

This game helps you get in touch with how you feel about certain issues. 'A', you start first, *keeping your eyes open,* and finish a sentence spontaneously as many times as you can in a few moments. Do not explain, give details or dialogue with your partner. Simply say the sentence over and over again, each time with a new ending. For example, "(Love) is . . . wonderful. (Love) is . . . precious. (Love) is . . . needed everywhere in the world."

'B', you simply give your partner your full attention, making eye contact and being a good listener.

Are there any questions ? Ready. Begin.

(Pause 1-2 minutes, then continue with the following instructions.)

Stop! Everyone stop. Now 'A', you repeat the same procedure, using the sentence, "(Sex) is . . ."

(Pause 1-2 minutes, then repeat the entire sequence with roles reversed, and finish with the following instructions.)

Stop! Everyone stop. Now take a few minutes to talk about what you have learned about yourself and your partner. Was any topic easier or more difficult for you? If so, does it say anything about how you deal with the topic in your life? What patterns did you notice about how your partner played the game?

FROZEN TAG
(Action and Silly Game)

(In large groups, a.variation after 2-3 minutes is to introduce a second person who is simultaneously 'It', or else the game may continue indefinitely).

In this tag game, you experience the value of cooperation and mutual support.

One person is 'It' who runs after people, trying to tag them. If you are tagged by the person who is 'It', you must stop and freeze in place. However, anyone who is not frozen may unfreeze you by crawling through your legs *(or alternatively, by shaking your hand.)*

Play continues until all participants but one are frozen.

Are there any questions? Ready. Begin.

(When everyone is finished, invite participants to talk about their experience with the exercise.)

GREETING DANCE
(Opening Game)

(Suggested music: 'Kos Greeting Dance' (Ena Mythos) from Spirit of Dance: The Next Steps *cassette tape, available from Findhorn Press.)*

Stand in a circle.

This dance is a greeting dance from the Greek island of Kos. It is said that wives of fishermen used this dance to greet their husbands when they returned after long absences at sea.

Take one step into the circle with your left foot. Then bring your right foot next to it, and make two little bounces or dips by bending your knees slightly. Now take one step backward with your right foot. Bring your left foot back to join it. Bounce twice again. Finally, take one step to the right *(anti-clockwise)* with your right foot. Bring your left foot next to it. Bounce twice again. Then repeat this sequence for the rest of the dance.

One interpretation of this dance is, 'As we step forward, we greet each other; as we step back, we give each other space; as we step to the side, we all move onward together.'

We join hands during this dance, so cross your hands over your chest (with your right arm *over* the left one) and take the left hand of the person to your left with your right hand while taking the right hand of the person to your right with your left hand. Do not lock your elbows in place, as it will tend to make you rigid. Keep your heart area open and your body loose.

As this is a dance of greeting, make eye contact with each person in the circle during the dance. Say hello to everyone with your eyes.

Are there any questions? Ready. Begin.

GROUP AGREEMENTS
(Preparing the Group)

A group functions more easily and effectively when its members agree to the conditions under which the group operates. The specific content of the agreements is not as important as the fact that *all* members of the group (and not just a majority) agree to support them.

When a new group forms, it is wise to take a few minutes to consider the factors members of the group value and are able to support. It is important that time is also given to discuss differences of opinion until, hopefully, group consensus (and not just a majority) can be reached.

Respect for individual differences and the need for everyone to feel included in the group help create win-win situations in which everyone gives and receives, and the group's purpose may then be achieved more easily. Making group agreements is an important step in building trust in a group and needs to be taken before presenting *Playful Self-Discovery*.

Typical Findhorn Foundation agreements often include the following:

1. We all agree to start and stop all sessions at the agreed time (whether or not everyone has arrived or can attend throughout the entire session), and to require everyone's agreement for any session to go overtime.

2. We all agree not to bring food or beverages into the room.

3. We all agree to give our full attention to the group by making eye contact with whoever is speaking.

4. We all agree to give all members of the group permission to express freely and clearly our thoughts, emotions and feelings.

5. We all agree to take responsibility for our own experience by making 'I' statements (i.e., saying 'I', not 'one', 'you', 'everybody', etc.).

6. We all agree to treat each other with respect.

7. We all agree to give and receive clear, open and honest feedback directly to each other and not talk behind each other's back.

8. We all agree to keep all personal disclosures in confidence.

9. We all agree to give our active support to the group (and not expect others to do everything for us), knowing we will get back from the group whatever time and effort we put into the group.

GROUP KNOT
(Close-Touching and Attunement Game)

Divide into groups of eight to ten people, and stand in a circle.

This game is an exercise in group cooperation and attunement.

Extend your arms and hands in front of you at shoulder height, parallel with the floor, and move into the circle until everyone's hands overlap. On the count of three, gently take a different hand in each of yours. Make sure they are not the hands of the same person, and, if possible, not the hands of people immediately on either side of you. One, two, three.

You have now formed a 'Group Knot', like a knotted shoelace. The object is to untangle yourselves without dropping hands. Attune to each other and find the best solution for untangling the whole group. You have ten minutes to untangle yourselves.

If you untangle yourselves right away, try it again.

Are there any questions? Ready. Begin.

(If a group continues to have difficulty after 6-8 minutes, make the following suggestion.)

If only two people who are now holding hands with each other were to drop their hands momentarily to help resolve your difficulty, which two people should it be? Attune to it, and then go ahead and do it.

(When everyone is finished, invite participants to talk about their experience with the exercise.)

GROUP SPIRAL
(Close-Touching and Closing Game)

Stand in a circle and join hands.

(The facilitator puts the person to his or her right in the centre of the circle, drops hands with that person only, and tells the person to stand still and not to move no matter what happens. With the rest of the group still joining hands, the facilitator then begins to walk in a circle in an anti-clockwise direction while participants slowly begin to wind around the person in the centre. Do not run or skip around as doing so usually pulls the circle too tightly together. When everyone is wound around each other, continue with the following instructions.)

Now for a brief moment, close your eyes. Begin to sense this group as a *group*. Experience it as a living, breathing *Being* all of its own. Feel yourself a part of it. Blend with it. Relax into it. For a moment longer, feel the spirit and the love of the group, and open yourself to giving and receiving this love, for what you have actually formed is a group hug!

(Pause 1 minute, then continue with the following instructions.)

Now the person in the centre, you drop down and crawl under everyone else so as to come outside and, without dropping hands, everyone follow along behind to come out into a large circle again.

(Once the large circle has re-formed, make the following point.)

This 'Group Spiral' demonstrates that whatever situation you may get yourself into, you can get yourself out of it as well!

(When everyone is finished, invite participants to talk about their experience with the exercise.)

GROUP STORY
(Creative and Attunement Game)

(Choose a title or theme for the story, for example, 'Play Each Day Keeps the Doctor Away' or 'Love Conquers All', or relate the game more directly to participants by suggesting they present a history of the group in fairy tale, mystery, science fiction, soap opera or other literary form.)

Sit quietly in a circle.

The purpose of this exercise is to attune to each other to create a group story.

One person begins by saying two or three sentences, ending in the middle of a sentence if you wish.

The next person in the circle continues with two or three more sentences, and so on and on, with each person adding to the story until it comes to an end.

(Depending upon the size of the group, go around the circle once or twice or more until a conclusion to the story is reached.)

(To conclude, invite participants to talk about their experience with the exercise.)

(A challenging variation is to create a group poem with each participant in turn contributing one or more lines.)

HAND-TO-HAND COMMUNICATION
(Trust and Attunement Game)

Stand in a circle. For this game, take off your rings, watches, bracelets and other hand jewellery. This game is called 'Hand-To-Hand Communication', and for it two groups of exactly equal size are needed, so go around the circle and each person count off one, two, one, two.

Ones, form a circle facing outward. Twos, form an outer circle around the Ones, facing inward towards the Ones.

The purpose of this game is to discover how much you can communicate with a partner *non-verbally*, using only the sense of touch and your intuition. It is a non-verbal exercise, so remain silent for the entire exercise. You will have time to talk about your experience with it later. It is also a trust game because you play it with your eyes closed. If you open your eyes at any time before the end, it will spoil the game for you. I will explain what to do next, once you begin. Are there any questions?

Members of each circle join hands with your own circle. Close your eyes. As I count, *each* circle take six steps to your right. One, two, three, four, five, six. Drop your hands. Keep your eyes closed while I move some of you in the outer circle so that you will be standing directly in front of your partner.

Now reach out and make contact with your *partner's hands only*. Focus only on your partner's hands during the whole exercise. Remember, remain silent, with no talking. Do not laugh or make a sound so your partner will not have a clue as to who you are . . . First explore the hands themselves . . . How large are they? . . . How rough or smooth? . . . How warm or cool? . . . How are the fingers and fingernails?

With your eyes closed, let your intuition tell you about your partner . . . Is your partner male or female? . . . How old is your partner? . . . What are some of your partner's basic qualities? . . . What else can you intuit about your partner? . . .

Keeping your eyes closed, discover how much you can express to your partner through your hands only. For example, use your hands to greet this person, to say hello to him or her silently through touch . . .

Now take a moment to express playfulness . . . Now express sadness . . . Now express impatience to your partner . . . Now express curiosity . . . Now express anger . . . Now express loneliness to your partner . . .

Those people in the outer circle, recall a time when you felt very loving towards someone and remember what that love feels like to you . . . Express this feeling of love to your partner now, through your hands only, without any conditions tied to it. And you people in the inner circle, open yourselves to receiving this unconditional love, love which asks nothing from you, no restrictions or expectations, love which is being expressed to you now just because you are you . . . Open your heart and *feel* it . . .

(Pause 1-2 minutes, then continue with the following instructions.)

Love is given to you so you may share it with others. So those people in the inner circle, take the love you have been receiving, and let it pour out to your partner without conditions. Those people in the outer circle, drop your protective barriers, open your heart and let this unconditional love come inside you now . . .

(Pause 1-2 minutes, then continue with the following instructions.)

It will soon be time to leave your partner, but before you do, keeping your eyes closed, express to your partner a personal quality as a parting gift, something to remember you by . . .

The time has come to say goodbye silently to your partner, through your hands only to your partner's hands only . . . Now drop your hands . . . When you are ready, open your eyes, and take a few minutes to talk about the experience with your partner.

(This exercise may be repeated immediately with everyone having a different partner. An alternative ending is to have participants in both circles join hands again before opening their eyes and move three steps to the right. Then ask them to open their eyes and find their original partners.)

HEAD, SHOULDERS, KNEES AND TOES
(Action and Silly Game)

(To the tune of 'There Is A Tavern In The Town')

First sing this song at a normal pace, using both hands to pat or point to your own specific body parts as they are sung.

Head, shoulders, knees and toes, knees and toes,
Head, shoulders, knees and toes, knees and toes.
And eyes and ears and mouth and nose,
Head, shoulders, knees and toes, knees and toes.

(Without stopping, continue repeating the song three or four times, going faster and faster each time.)

Now sing it again at a normal pace, including the gestures.

The next time through the song, omit singing the word 'Head', but pat your head with both hands as usual, and then continue singing the rest of the song. The following time through the song, omit singing the words 'Head' and 'Shoulders', but pat them as usual, and then continue singing the rest of the song. And so on and on until the whole song is 'sung' without words but with pats and gestures alone.

(Once in Germany, the author presented this song in a group, after which one of the participants said, "I am amazed. I am a kindergarten teacher, and I have always done this song with my children. I didn't know it could be done with adults!" The author replied mischievously, "I too am amazed. I am an adult group leader, and I have always done this song with grown-ups. I didn't know it could be done with children!")

HUG TAG
(Action and Silly Game)

(A small cushion or pillow is required for this game.)

This light and active game helps show your interdependence with each other. It is a tag game with a person who is 'It', trying to tag someone else, who then becomes 'It'. The person who is 'It' carries a cushion or pillow under the arm so that everyone else knows who is 'It'.

In tag games there is sometimes a safe place where you can keep from being tagged. As this game is called 'Hug Tag', the safe place is when you are hugging someone else.

All hugs must be proper hugs, that is, face-to-face and belly-to-belly embraces, with both partners having both arms around each other.

You may hug someone for only five seconds, then you must release the hug and find someone else to hug. The person who is 'It' cannot wait around for the five seconds to pass to tag someone, but must keep moving. The person who is 'It' must tag only with your hand. Do not tag with the cushion, as otherwise someone's glasses could be broken. Simply keep the cushion under your arm as the sign that you are 'It'.

Are there any questions? Ready. Begin.

(When everyone is finished, invite participants to talk about their experience with the exercise. Later, make the following point.)

How did you play the game? Were you aware that you had a choice, either to run *away* from whoever is 'It', or to run *towards* someone to hug, and thus save someone else while you saved yourself from being tagged?

*(As a variation in larger groups, after 2-3 minutes add a second cushion so that a second person becomes simultaneously 'It'. Another variation is to stop the action after 2-3 minutes long enough to say that now to be safe, everyone must hug **two** other people at a time!)*

HUMAN SPRING
(Trust and Attunement Game)

Choose a partner and stand facing each other.

This game, called 'Human Spring', is a test of your trust and attunement.

Put your hands up in front of you, close to your chest, palms facing outward. Attune to each other, and when it feels right to you both, fall forward towards each other. Time your fall so that you each meet in the centre of the space between the two of you. Then simultaneously give each other a tiny push back so that you both return to an upright and balanced position.

Next take a *small* step backward (because two small steps make one big step!), and try it again and again, until you reach the limit of your distance apart.

The object of the game is not to try to trick each other into becoming off-balanced, but rather to attune to and help each other in a coordinated way, as two parts of a greater whole working harmoniously together.

After you have reached your limits with one partner, find another partner and try it again.

Are there any questions? Ready. Begin.

(When everyone is finished, invite participants to talk about their experience with the exercise.)

HUMLESS
(Silly and Trust Game)

(Either choose to be the 'Humless' yourself, or once the game begins tap someone on the shoulder to be the 'Humless'.)

The name of this game is 'Humless', and it is a game of trust and intuition.

Get down on your hands and knees, close your eyes and begin crawling around the floor, humming. One person is secretly designated to be the 'Humless' who remains standing with legs apart and does not hum.

Your task is to find the 'Humless' and when you do, to crawl between his or her legs *from the front only* (to avoid any collisions), then stand up, stop humming, open your eyes, put your hands on the waist of the person and begin to form a chain of the 'Humless' one.

Are there any questions? Ready. Begin.

(When everyone is finished, invite participants to talk about their experience with the exercise.)

I BLESS YOU, I TRUST YOU, I SUPPORT YOU
(Attunement and Closing Game)

(Suggested music: 'The Magic Flute,' *by Jan Prinz, available from Findhorn Press. This exercise is recommended to be used in new groups which will be together for some while, in an early meeting to help lay the groundwork for their time together.)*

Everyone stand.

This exercise gives you the opportunity of making a close contact with each person in the group.

When the music starts, approach someone, take his or her hands in yours, make eye contact, and calling the person by name, say "__(Name)__, I bless you, I trust you, I support you."

Then the other person, you say the same thing back to your partner. When both of you have finished, if you wish, give each other a brief hug, and then move on to someone else. Do not say anything else or dialogue with anyone. You can always do that another time.

If you are not sure you sincerely feel or believe the words in every case, it does not matter. Let it be a statement of *intention* on your part. Keep moving. Take no more than one minute for the two of you together before moving on to the next person.

Do not turn the exercise into a mechanical ritual. Keep it fresh. Feel the feelings behind the words. Feel it as much as you can, as you say it and as you hear it from the other person. Stay open to give to and receive from each other in this way. When you have met everyone in the room, then sit down.

Are there any questions? Ready. Begin.

(When everyone is finished, invite participants to talk about their experience with the exercise.)

ICE-BREAKER
(Preparing the Group and Name Game)

Everyone stand.

It is often reassuring when a new group begins to form for everyone to know straight away who all the people are in the group, where they are from and something about each one of them. It is helpful for everyone to make a brief personal contact with each other early on *(within the first hour)* and to be able to greet each other in a friendly fashion. This exercise is such an 'Ice-Breaker'.

Begin to circulate around the room. Approach someone (taking his or her hands in yours, if it feels right to you) and say, "Hello, my name is __(David)__, I am from __(London)__ and my star sign is __(Taurus)__." Then the other person, you tell your partner the same information about yourself.

Then each of you move on to find another person. Continue until you have met everyone in the room. It is not the time to engage in conversation or tell everyone the story of your life, just your name, where you are from and your star sign. When you have met everyone in the room, then sit down.

Are there any questions? Ready. Begin.

(Once everyone is seated, ask by a show of hands how many people represent the twelve signs of the zodiac: Aries, Taurus, Gemini, Cancer, Leo, Virgo, Libra, Scorpio, Sagittarius, Capricorn, Aquarius and Pisces. Also, as a point of interest, ask if everyone remembers which group member lives nearest to the meeting place and which one lives farthest away.)

(An alternative to the star sign is to use 'My favourite food is . . .')

I IMAGINE
(Preparing the Group and Attunement Game)

(This exercise demonstrates the great extent to which all people are able to attune to and intuit objective information about each other. Accordingly, it should be done the first day a new group meets, before people become acquainted with each other. If appropriate for the group, it may be used as an 'Ally Exercise'.*)*

Choose a partner, someone you do not know. Decide who is 'A' and who is 'B'. Sit quietly facing each other and make eye contact with each other for this exercise called 'I Imagine'.

'A', take a moment to become quiet, clearing your mind as much as possible, and letting it become like a blank screen. Then, keeping eye contact with your partner, begin to make a series of short statements about 'B', all beginning with the words, 'I imagine . . . .' Let specific images or ideas come to you to describe your partner. Do not *think* about it, just *imagine* it. And because you are imagining it, you do not have to worry about whether you are right or wrong. Remember, you are not guessing. You are simply imagining what your partner is like.

For example, you might say, "I imagine you have never married. I imagine you enjoy being out in nature, especially the seashore. I imagine you prefer to read non-fiction rather than fiction. I imagine you get up early and go to bed early. I imagine you feel close to animals, especially dogs. I imagine you like Italian-style cooking," and so on.

'B', you are just a good listener and say nothing. Your task is to be warm and friendly and supportive, but do not show any reaction to whatever your partner may say about you. Try not to give your partner any outward clues as to the accuracy of his or her statements. Be completely neutral until you each have had a turn.

After a few minutes I will say 'Stop', and then you will reverse roles. When each of you has had a turn, you will have time to talk about your experience.

Are there any questions? Ready. Begin.

(Pause 3-5 minutes, then continue with the following instructions.)

Stop! Everyone stop. Now reverse roles. 'B' imagines what 'A' is like, and 'A' is the good listener. Remember, do not worry about getting it right or wrong. Your task is simply to let your imagination flow. Ready. Begin.

(Pause 3-5 minutes, then continue with the following instructions.)

Stop! Everyone stop. Now take a few minutes to talk with your partner about your experience with this exercise.

(Pause 6-8 minutes, then invite participants to talk about their experience in the group. Conclude the exercise by making the following point.)

This exercise demonstrates that everyone is an 'open book' for each other (even for relative strangers) to read easily and accurately. It suggests that you might as well live your life as openly and honestly as you can if people who wish to take the time and effort can know so much about you anyway!

LAP SIT
(Trust and Close-Touching Game)

Stand in a circle with someone the same size as you on either side of you.

We can do many things as a group which we cannot do as individuals, and this game, called 'Lap Sit', is one of them. It tests how trusting you are. Everyone turn facing to the right *(anti-clockwise)*. Step in closer to the centre, and stand so you can put your hands on the waist of the person in front of you. In a moment, we each are going to sit on the knees of the person behind us, keeping our own knees together as we do.

Your task is to guide the person in front of you to sit comfortably on your knees, and not to worry about whether you are going to make it safely to the knees of the person behind you! Concentrate on the person in front of you, and trust the person behind to guide you safely.

We will have a trial run first. On the count of three, we are going to bend down, touch bottoms to knees and come right back up to make sure we are all standing closely enough together. One, two, three.

(Go down and touch, then come right up again and make any necessary adjustments. Often participants are not standing in a perfect circle, or they are not standing closely enough together with their toes touching the heels of the person in front of them.)

On the count of three we actually are going to sit down and remain seated. Are there any questions? Ready. One, two, three.

(Once seated, slowly release and extend one hand, then the other.)

Let's walk together! On the count of three, everyone pick up your right foot and move it forward. One, two, three. Now pick up and move your left foot forward. One, two, three. *(Repeat.)* Finally, on the count of three, we will all get up together. One, two, three.

It is said this game was originally called 'Empress Eugenie's Circle' from the Austrian empress's account of how her soldiers kept dry while resting in a wet field awaiting a royal visit.

LEARNING TO SEE EACH OTHER*
(Exploration and Attunement Game)

Choose a partner, someone you do not know very well, if at all. Sit quietly facing each other, holding hands. It is a non-verbal exercise, so remain silent for the entire exercise. You will have time to talk about your experience with it later.

So often we do not take the time or trouble to truly experience others, to see them as they really are and to make an authentic connection with them. This exercise, called 'Learning to See Each Other', gives you the opportunity to make contact with another human being.

Take a few deep breaths, breathing out tension and centring yourself . . . Look into each other's eyes . . . If you feel discomfort or an urge to laugh or look away, just note your embarrassment with patience and gentleness towards yourself and come back, when you can, to your partner's eyes . . .

Allow the awareness to come to you that you may never see this person again after today . . . The opportunity to behold the uniqueness of this particular human being is given to you now . . .

As you look into this being's eyes, let yourself become aware of the powers which are there . . . Open yourself to awareness of the gifts and strengths and the potentialities in this being . . . Behind those eyes are unmeasured reserves of ingenuity and endurance, of wit and wisdom . . . There are gifts there, of which this person is unaware . . . Consider what these untapped powers can do for the healing of our planet and the relishing of our common life . . .

As you do, let yourself become aware of your desire for this person to be free from fear . . . Let yourself experience how much you want this being to be free from hatred . . . Free from sorrow . . . Free from the causes of suffering . . . Know that what you are now experiencing is the great loving-kindness . . . It is good for building a world . . .

Now as you look into those eyes, let yourself become aware of the pain which is there . . . There are sorrows accumulated in that life's journey . . . There are griefs and losses, hurts and disappointments beyond the telling, as in all human lives . . . Let yourself open to them . . . You cannot take the pain away, cannot 'fix' it, but you *can* be unafraid to be with it . . . Know that what you are now experiencing is the great compassion . . . It is good for healing our world . . .

As you look into those eyes, let yourself become aware of the love which is there as a divine birthright . . . Open yourself to the vast reservoir of unconditional love available to all of us to be given freely, fully and fearlessly . . .

As you look into those eyes, open to the thought of how good it would be to make common cause . . . Consider how ready you might be to work together, to take risks in a joint venture . . . Imagine the zest of doing that, the excitement and laughter of engaging on a common project, acting boldly and trusting each other . . . As you open to this possibility, know that what you open to is the great wealth: the pleasure in each other's powers, the joy in each other's joy . . .

Lastly now, let your awareness drop deep, deep within you, below the level of what words can express . . . Open to the deep web of relationship which underlies and interweaves all experiencing, all knowing . . . It is the web of life in which you have taken being and in which you are supported . . . Out of that vast web you cannot fall . . . For that vast web is what you are . . . Feel the assurance of that knowledge . . . Feel the great peace . . . Rest in it . . . From that great peace, you can venture everything . . . You can trust . . . You can act . . . You can love . . .

(Pause 1-2 minutes, then continue with the following instructions.)

Now take a few minutes to be with one another, and, if you wish, to talk about your experience with this exercise.

*Adapted from *Despair and Personal Power In The Nuclear Age,* by Joanna Rogers Macy, Ph.D. ISBN 0-86571-031-7

MEDITATION DANCE
(Attunement and Closing Game)

(Suggested music: 'Pachelbel's Canon', *available from the Phoenix Shop, Findhorn Foundation. This dance is a quiet way to bring* Playful Self-Discovery *to a close while keeping the group together.)*

Stand in a circle.

This simple dance is a 'Meditation Dance'.

Turn to the right *(anti-clockwise)*. Put your right hand on the left shoulder of the person in front of you. Take three steps forward beginning with the right foot. Then without lifting your foot off the floor, simply rock back on your left heel. Take three more steps forward beginning with your right foot and rock back on the left. Continue this sequence until the end of the dance. Allow the music to guide you.

It is said that this dance is from the Knights Templars and the weight of the hand on the shoulder symbolises the weight of the cross which Jesus Christ carried. Another explanation is that the three steps forward symbolise expansion and the one step back, consolidation. Still another interpretation is that the dance symbolises the four seasons, with the step back being winter.

You may close your eyes if you wish, but hold the *entire group* in your awareness to help bring to an end all of the group activities, insights, feelings and thoughts you have experienced during the *Playful Self-Discovery* session today.

Are there any questions? Ready. Begin.

(When the dance is finished, invite participants to talk about their experience with it.)

MIRRORING
(Creative and Attunement Game)

(Suggested music: The Magic Flute' *by Jan Prinz, available from Findhorn Press.)*

Choose a partner you do not know very well. Decide who is 'A' and who is 'B' and stand facing each other. This game, called 'Mirroring', is a non-verbal exercise, so remain silent for the entire exercise. You will have time to talk about your experience with it later.

When the music starts, 'A', you slowly begin to move your hands and arms in gentle gestures, later moving your torso, head, legs and the rest of your body in any way you choose. 'B', you *simultaneously* mirror 'A's actions, replicating every movement in the same moment.

Begin slowly until you have established good contact with each other. The object is not to try to trick the person doing the mirroring, but to establish a creative flow between you. Eye contact is helpful, but expand your awareness to include your partner's entire body. Are there any questions? Ready. Begin.

(Pause 2-3 minutes, then continue with the following instructions.)

Change roles, with 'B' taking the lead and 'A' doing the mirroring.

(Pause 2-3 minutes, then continue with the following instructions.)

Now neither one of you leads all of the time. Allow the initiative to come from a common attunement and passes back and forth between you.

(Pause 2-3 minutes, then continue with the following instructions.)

Move into groups of four where your movements relate in harmony. Gradually merge with other groups until the entire group has come together in a circle, and you all continue to move together in harmony.

(Pause 2-3 minutes, then conclude by inviting participants to talk about their experience with the exercise.)

MORNING ROUTINE
(Silly and Creative Game)

(Keep each person's action short, 30 seconds or less, or this game may take a long time. Or, use it only in groups of 8-12 people).

Form a semi-circle or horseshoe pattern, with the space in the open side to be used as a stage.

This game draws upon your skills of observation and creativity. For this mime performance everyone contributes something, silently acting out a portion of your usual morning routine. It is a non-verbal exercise, so remain silent for the entire exercise. You will have time to talk about your experience with it later.

For example, the first person to start the mime moves into the open space of the semi-circle, lies on the floor in front of the group as if asleep, hears the alarm clock sounding, throws back the bed clothes, and hops out of bed (or however else your morning usually begins) and then stops the performance at that point and returns to the semi-circle.

The next person *repeats* this action and then *adds* another short action of what might typically follow in his or her own morning routine, such as exercising, showering, dressing, preparing breakfast and so on.

Each person repeats *all* actions which have gone before and then adds a brief contribution to the mime.

Are there any questions? Ready. Begin.

(When everyone is finished, invite participants to talk about their experience with the exercise.)

MOVING STATUES
(Creative and Attunement Game)

(Refer to the front cover for one artist's impression of this game.)
Divide into groups of 6-8 people.

One person from the first group, either standing, sitting or lying on the floor, assumes the position of a working machine part (such as a pendulum, flywheel, or piston), swinging, stomping, or rocking one or more parts of your body rhythmically and making an appropriate sound to accompany the action.

After a long moment to allow everyone to appreciate and attune to whatever the person is doing, a second person joins the first one, and adds a new complementary or opposing action and sound.

Then after a short while, a third person joins them, and on and on with *one person at a time* slowly and deliberately joining them until all members of the group are engaged in an overall integrated action.

The other groups then walk about the creation, admiring it from all sides, in the end applauding its originality and creativity.

Then a person from the next group starts a new statue and the process begins again, until each group has formed an interconnected, coordinated 'Moving Statue', which is the name of this game.

Are there any questions? Ready. Begin.

(When everyone is finished, invite participants to talk about their experience with the exercise.)

NAME CHAIN
(Opening and Name Game)

(This is the fastest, most effective way the author has found for a group to learn everyone's name, owing both to the repetition of names and to people's earnest motivation to listen carefully to each name because they know they have to repeat it. Groups of up to 12 participants may do this game standing, but larger groups may wish to sit. The larger the group, the more essential it is to do a name game of some sort. The author has used this game in meetings of 40 people with great success.)

Form a circle.

The first step in creating a safe and friendly group is to become better acquainted with each other. One way to start the process is to learn each other's name.

This game is called 'Name Chain', and I will start by saying "Hello! My name is __(David)__." Then the person to my right will say "Hello! My name is __(Eileen)__, and this is my friend, __(David)__." Then the person to her right will say "Hello! My name is __(Peter)__, and these are my friends, __(Eileen and David)__," and so on and on around the circle until the person on my left repeats everyone's name.

Always repeat the names in the same order each time, starting with the newest name added and ending with the name of the very first person. Are there any questions? Ready. Begin.

(When everyone is finished, invite participants to talk about their experience with the exercise.)

(As a point of honour, the person who starts the game, usually the facilitator, should conclude the game by reciting all of the names. Often the participants will expect it of you, so do be prepared!)

(A variation is to go around the circle a second time with everyone adding descriptive qualities of themselves, for example, "Hello, I am fun-loving David," which then everyone repeats.)

NAME MANTRA
(Opening and Name Game)

Stand in a large circle.

In this game called 'Name Mantra', the first person steps forward and you tell the group your name, at the same time making a sweeping gesture or movement which is expressive of who you are or how you are feeling at the moment.

The whole group then repeats your name and gesture three times, exactly as you did it, while you stand back silently and receive the group's reflection.

Are there any questions? Ready. Begin.

(When everyone is finished, invite participants to talk about their experience with the exercise.)

NICKNAMES
(Name and Exploration Game)

(The effectiveness of this game may vary from country to country as some nationalities tend to use nicknames more than others. Also be aware that this simple exercise may trigger surprising emotional associations and memories for participants.)

Form a circle for a game called 'Nicknames'.

Throughout our lives most of us have been called a variety of nicknames by our family, friends, schoolmates, co-workers, lovers and others. Some of the names may be amusing and descriptive, others may be affectionate and quite intimate and still others may be not so nice at all.

Let us go round the circle, and each person take a few moments simply to say to the group the different nicknames you have been called during your lifetime. No need to give any explanations or details. It is perfectly fine if you experience and express any feelings associated with the names you remember, or with the people who used them. End your listing with the name you want to be called in this group.

Are there any questions? Ready. Begin.

(When everyone is finished, invite participants to talk about their experience with the exercise.)

(As a variation, to intensify the game, after a participant says each nickname, the group repeats it back to the person.)

PEOPLE PASS
(Trust and Close-Touching Game)

(This game is more effective with groups of 15-30 people.)

Divide into two equal groups. Stand in two lines closely together, with everyone facing the same direction towards one end.

This game, called 'People Pass', is a test of your balance, co-ordination and trust.

The first person at the end of one line leans back and is gently picked up and held in a horizontal position parallel to the ground by the group and is passed slowly along at waist height to the other end of the line, and then is carefully put down and takes a new position at the far end of the line.

Then the next person at the opposite end of the other line leans back and is picked up, and on and on until everyone has been passed down the line.

Are there any questions? Ready. Begin.

(When everyone is finished, invite participants to talk about their experience with the exercise.)

PEOPLE-TO-PEOPLE
(Silly and Close-Touching Game)

Choose a partner.

As the first caller without a partner, I will call out two different parts of the body, such as 'back to back', and each partner then moves around so that both your backs are in contact with each other.

Or I might call out other interesting combinations such as 'nose to toes', 'elbows to knees', or 'ears to ankles', and each of you makes sure *both* of you are touching each other as indicated.

After three or four such positions, I will call out the name of this game, 'People-to-People', and then everyone has to find a new partner quickly. The person left without a partner becomes the new caller.

Are there any questions? Ready. Begin.

(When finished, invite participants to talk about their experience with the exercise.)

PERSONAL INTRODUCTIONS
(Preparing the Group)

Playful Self-Discovery is designed to foster openness and trust in groups. A useful starting point in this process is for all participants to introduce themselves to the group. Whether it is a new group or an established one where everyone knows each other, all participants need to present themselves, talk about themselves, take risks in revealing themselves and be seen by the group. The more open, honest and authentic they can be, the faster safety and trust develop in the group.

When preparing for *Playful Self-Discovery,* the author often gives people at least three opportunities to talk about themselves within the first four hours of a new group by using the 'Ice-Breaker' (playful and light with the whole group), 'Ally Exercise' (going deeper with just one other person) and 'Personal Introductions' (going deeper still in front of the whole group.) Refer to 'Preparation Session' pages 21-22. This self-disclosing process then continues in the *Playful Self-Discovery* session.

For 'Personal Introductions', chairs are arranged in a horseshoe pattern. Participants decide spontaneously when to introduce themselves by taking their place standing in front of the group at the open end of the horseshoe. They are all encouraged to take a risk of some kind in talking about themselves. The facilitator keeps track of time and advises speakers when five minutes have elapsed, after which time they are asked to finish and receive the applause of the group for introducing themselves and taking a risk.

Participants might wish to include the following points:
1. Their name and where they live
2. An interesting fact or two about themselves, perhaps something about their work, hobby, family and so on
3. Why they have come to the group, and what they would like to get from it, that is, their needs and expectations
4. What they are willing to give to the group: qualities, skills, time and so on
5. What fears, questions or concerns they have about the group
6. What they need from the group to feel comfortable being a member of it, such as clarity, confidentiality, honesty, respect and so on.

PICTURE POST CARDS
(Creative and Exploration Game)

(This psychosynthesis exercise requires a large number of picture post cards, from 100-300. The best source of such post cards are art galleries and museums, for their stock presents the human condition in a wide variety of ages, moods, conditions and situations, literally, and also symbolically with representations of animals, objects, landscapes and abstract designs.)

(Place post cards on the floor face up so that they all may be seen, which is best done either before the session begins or during a break so that participants see them when they first come into the room. Play appropriate music in the background later during the time participants walk around displaying their post cards.)

This non-verbal exercise bypasses the cognitive mind and engages other parts of yourself, so remain silent for the entire exercise. You will have time to talk about your experience with it later.

Walk around the post cards and carefully note each one.

(Pause 2-3 minutes, then continue with the following instructions.)

Continue to move around the cards,* and now allow your attention to be attracted by one or two of them in particular.

(Pause 2-3 minutes, then continue with the following instructions.)

Now select one post card and pick it up. If someone takes your first choice before you can reach it, then select your second choice. Hold the post card at chest height facing outward so that everyone may see it, and walk slowly around the room observing each other's cards.

(Pause 2-3 minutes, then continue with the following instructions.)

Choose a partner and take a few minutes to talk about the particular quality or meaning this card has for you, and also how you experienced seeing other people and their cards.

*(*As a variation, this exercise may be used to prompt participants to project their feelings onto the cards in response to a question asked of them at the * in the instructions above. If using the*

exercise in this way, select a question to ask from the list below, or tailor one to the group, and continue with the following instructions.)

Now allow your attention to be attracted by one or two post cards in particular which literally depict or symbolically represent to you:

1. How you are feeling today
2. How you feel about this group
3. How you relate to this group
4. How you feel about (authority, commitment, death, men, women, money, sex, success, failure, responsibility, taking risks, work)
5. How you (underestimate yourself, overestimate yourself, would like to appear to others, imagine others expect you to be, would like to be, ideally)
6. What you like most about yourself, what you like least about yourself
7. Your (needs, wants, strengths, weaknesses, skills, doubts, fears)
8. Your (childhood, adolescence, adulthood, middle age, old age)
9. Your (past, present, future, next step — as related to a specific topic, issue or situation)
10. Your (purpose in life, greatest challenge in life, greatest disappointment in life, greatest joy in life)
11. Your secret (ambitions, desires, dreams, fantasies, goals)
12. The part of yourself you never show to anyone else

(Until you can build up a good supply of post cards, a variation which takes much more time is to provide a large stack of old magazines to the group, with at least one or two magazines for each participant. Also required are scissors, glue or paste and large sheets of paper for everyone. Select and ask the relevant question(s) above. Participants then scan through the magazines looking for photographs, artwork, headlines and other features which represent answers to the questions, and which they cut out and paste on to a large sheet of paper provided to each person. Participants choose a partner and talk about their experience with the exercise.)

PILLOW TOSS
(Opening and Name Game)

(A small pillow or cushion is required for this game.)

Stand in a circle for a game called 'Pillow Toss'.

To help everyone learn each other's names, I will start by telling the group my name and then choose the person who goes next by tossing a pillow to him or her. That person tells the group his or her name, then chooses someone else and tosses the pillow to that person.

(After all participants have said their names to the group once or twice, continue with the following instructions.)

Now to reinforce the names, I will call out the name of a person and then toss the pillow to that person, who then calls out the name of another person and then tosses the pillow to that person, until we have heard each other's names again.

(Complete the game after everyone's name has been called out once or twice.)

(When finished, invite participants to talk about their experience with the exercise.)

PLANETS
(Trust, Attunement and Closing Game)

(Suggested music: 'Oxygene' by Jean Michel Jarre, available from the Phoenix Shop, Findhorn Foundation.)

Find your own space in the room, and stand quietly with your eyes closed.

The name of this psychosynthesis exercise is 'Planets', and it is a trust game which helps you to know more about yourself and others. It is a non-verbal exercise, so remain silent for the entire exercise. You will have time to talk about your experience with it later.

(Start the music quietly in the background.)

Move your attention to inside yourself. Experience your body . . . Your emotions . . . Your thoughts . . . Feel yourself as a separate and complete being, a universe unto yourself . . .

Now allow your imagination to give you a sense of yourself as a planet in space . . . What do you look like as a planet? . . . What is your shape? . . . What is your size? . . . What does your surface look like, that part you show to the rest of the universe? . . . What are your predominant features? . . .

Go beneath the surface to the first level under it . . . What is it like? . . . What is going on there? . . . What do you see? . . .

Move to the next level below that one, going deeper into your planet . . . What is it like? . . . What is going on there? . . . What do you see? . . .

Now, move to the very centre of your essence . . . What is it like? . . . What is going on there? . . . What do you see? . . .

(Either invite participants to open their eyes, choose a partner and take 3-5 minutes each to talk about their experience of themselves as a planet before moving into the second part of the exercise, or continue with the following instructions.)

Next, having explored the inner planet, with your eyes closed, imagine yourself as your planet moving through the vast reaches of outer space . . . As you do, begin to move about the room keeping your awareness within yourself. Imagine everyone else in the group, all the other planets, moving about separately, isolated from one another. If you come close to anyone else, move away. Do not make contact . . . Continue feeling how it is to be separate from everyone else . . .

(Pause 1-2 minutes, then continue with the following instructions.)

Slowly begin to move your awareness outward, still keeping your eyes closed, but now when you come into contact with others, greet them and welcome them into your space, and then move on . . . Continue moving about, feeling what it is like to extend your universe outward to include others . . . Imagine others doing it as well . . .

(Pause 1-2 minutes, then continue with the following instructions.)

Now as you continue to move through space, when you come into contact with another planet, reach out, embrace it and begin to move together to form a cluster of planets, slowly uniting with all the others into one vast solar system . . .

(Pause 1-2 minutes, then after the group has come together, continue with the following instructions.)

Attune to the cluster and see what it is like . . . Experience how it feels to be part of a larger wholeness . . . Experience how it feels to be interconnected with everyone and everything in the universe . . .

(Pause 1-2 minutes, then continue with the following instructions.)

Now allow to come to you a quality within yourself to share with this group of planets, your personal contribution or gift to them . . .

(Pause 1-2 minutes, then continue with the following instructions.)

When you feel ready, open your eyes and make contact with the other planets in your solar system, and begin to radiate to them the special quality you have chosen to give them.

(Pause 1-2 minutes, then conclude either by inviting the participants to talk about their experience with the exercise, or by having a group hug.)

PRUI
(Silly and Trust Game)

(Either choose to be the 'Prui', or once the game begins tap some-one on the shoulder to be the 'Prui'.)

The name of this game is 'Prui' *(PROO-ee)*, the name of a mythical monster who does not talk. It is a game of trust and intuition.

One person is secretly designated to be the 'Prui' who stands still and says nothing.

Everyone else walks slowly around the room with your eyes closed searching for the 'Prui'. When you encounter someone, ask, "Prui?" If the other person is *not* the 'Prui', that person responds by saying, "Prui."

As the 'Prui' remains silent, when you find someone who does not respond, then you know you have found the 'Prui'. Join hands with the 'Prui', open your eyes and begin to form a chain of the 'Prui'.

Are there any questions? Ready. Begin.

(To conclude, invite participants to talk about their experi-ence with the exercise.)

RAIN
(Attunement Game)

(This game helps to quiet an overactive or high-energy group.)

Sit quietly in a circle.

This game is called 'Rain' because of the sounds created while playing it. It is a non-verbal game, so remain silent.

As I turn slowly around in the centre of the circle, I will make a gesture. As I make eye contact with each of you, begin to repeat the gesture I make and continue it until the next time I make eye contact with you and the gesture changes.

(For the first time around the circle, slowly tap one index finger against the other. For the next revolution, tap two fingers of one hand against two fingers of the other; then tap three fingers of one hand against three fingers of the other; then tap four fingers of one hand against four fingers of the other; then snap your fingers, then clap both hands together. With each succeeding revolution, increase the tempo and the loudness, so as to simulate the sound of more and more rain.)

(Then reverse the sequence until the final revolution silences all participants, and the rain has stopped!)

(To conclude, invite participants to talk about their experience with the exercise.)

SENSUALITY WALK
(Trust and Exploration Game)

Choose a partner, and decide who is 'A' and who is 'B'.

The purpose of this exercise, called 'Sensuality Walk', is to give you experience of your other senses without vision to aid you. It is a non-verbal exercise, so remain silent for the entire exercise. You will have time to talk about your experience with it later.

'A', you close your eyes. 'B', you keep your eyes open and take your partner by the hand to experience with as many senses as possible various objects in the room. 'B', stop 'A' from time to time near an object, perhaps a wall fixture, furniture, plants, even other people, and allow your partner to touch, listen to, smell or taste it. After a few minutes I will say, "Stop," and then you will reverse roles.

Are there any questions? Ready. Begin.

(Pause 3-5 minutes, then continue with the following instructions.)

Stop! Everyone stop. Without talking, now 'B', you close your eyes and 'A', you begin to lead 'B' around the room to different objects to be experienced with the senses.

(Pause 3-5 minutes, then continue with the following instructions.)

Stop! Everyone stop. Now take a few minutes to talk about your experience with the exercise, both as guide and as experiencer.

(If time and the floor plan allow, a variation is to let participants leave the room and explore other parts of the building, but for safety's sake only if no stairs have to be used. Another variation, if the weather and environs allow, is to let participants go outside into the surrounding landscape. With either of these variations, 'B' is told to watch the time and to reverse roles when half the time is left. For these variations allow from 10-20 minutes per person, and, as the exercise is longer, provide one blindfold for each couple if possible. After the second round, everyone returns to the room to process and conclude the exercise.)

SENTENCE COMPLETION
(Action and Silly Game)

(Suggested music: any lively contemporary music. Use sentences to prompt participants to open themselves to each other, such as "What I like most about being here is . . . ", "What I like most about myself is . . . ", "What I like least about myself is . . . ", "What I want most out of life is . . . ", "My biggest challenge in life is . . . ", and "What no one else knows about me is . . ." This exercise also easily lends itself to relating to the theme or purpose of the group.)

This game, called 'Sentence Completion', reveals how spontaneous you can be, and also it gives you the chance to dance.

When the music stops, find two other people, join hands, and listen to the first part of a sentence which I will say. Then allow something to come into your mind spontaneously to complete the sentence, and say it immediately to your group. When everyone in your group has completed the sentence, drop hands so that I know when everyone is ready to continue. When the music starts again, begin dancing. Later, when it stops, find two other people and listen to hear the first part of the next sentence as before.

Are there any questions? Ready. Begin.

(When everyone is finished, invite participants to talk about their experience with the exercise.)

SHOULDER MASSAGE
(Trust and Close-Touching Game)

Stand in a circle with someone the same size as you on either side of you.

Turn to the right *(anti-clockwise)*. Put your hands on the shoulders of the person in front of you. Now give that person the best shoulder massage he or she has ever had. Begin by rubbing the person gently and only become more vigorous if you feel it is what the person wants.

(Pause 2-3 minutes, then continue with the following instructions.)

Now turn around and thank the person who has just given you a massage by giving him or her the best massage that person has ever had.

(To conclude, invite participants to talk about their experience with the exercise.)

STAND UP
(Trust and Attunement Game)

(For proper traction, this game is best done on a carpeted floor.)

Choose a partner who is the same size as you, and sit on the floor back to back.

This game tests your trust, coordination and attunement.

Both partners interlock your arms. Bend your knees so that your feet are flat against the floor, close to your bottom. Silently attune to your partner, and when it feels right to you both, simultaneously press against each other's back while pushing downward with your feet. When you both do it together, you help each other to 'Stand Up', which is the name of this game.

The key is to sit closely to each other and put your backs squarely against one another. Also, both of you must press backward and downward at the same time, and as quickly as possible, once you start.

After you have been able to 'Stand Up' at least twice with the same partner, find another partner and try it again.

Are there any questions? Ready. Begin.

(When everyone is finished, invite participants to talk about their experience with the exercise.)

TRUST FALL
(Trust and Close-Touching Game)

Divide into groups of 8-10 people and, standing closely together, form a tight circle.

One person stands in the middle of the circle in a relaxed manner, with arms across your chest, hands on your shoulders and eyes closed. Allow yourself to lean or fall into the others, and let them roll you gently around the circle for a few moments in one direction and then the other. Everyone takes a turn in the circle.

Are there any questions? Ready. Begin.

(When everyone is finished, invite participants to talk about their experience with the exercise, either with their partners or in the group.)

(A variation is for participants to bless the person being rolled around in the middle by whispering a continuous round of qualities, such as Beauty, Clarity, Courage, Freedom, Inspiration, Joy, Love, Peace, Strength, Understanding and so on.)

TRUST WALK
(Trust Game)

Stand in a circle as large as the room permits.

The person who goes first, you close your eyes and without hesitation walk confidently across the circle. When you reach the other side of the circle, the nearest person stops you, turns you around, and gives you a little push into a new direction.

You then walk briskly off in the new direction, still with your eyes closed, and continue to crisscross the circle in this way several times. After a few minutes, someone else takes your place, until everyone has had a turn to 'Trust Walk', which is the name of this game.

Are there any questions? Ready. Begin.

(When everyone is finished, invite participants to talk about their experience with the exercise.)

UNFOLDING (IN PAIRS)
(Close-Touching and Attunement Game)

(Suggested music: 'Cavatina' *by John Williams. If the floor is not carpeted, provide a blanket for each couple. As you demonstrate the exercise, do so with the speed and sensitivity you would like participants to use. Do not rush it, or else they will too.)*

Choose a partner, someone you have not been with yet today. Decide who is 'A' and who is 'B'. Move to your own space in the room.

'A', you get down on the floor, close your eyes and curl yourself up into the most restricted, tightly-enclosed position imaginable, so you feel isolated, alienated and cut off from the rest of the world. As you do, allow any feelings, memories, images or thoughts to come to you.

The object of this non-verbal game, called 'Unfolding', is for 'B' to attune to 'A' *in total silence* and very lovingly help your partner to unfold into a new life of safety, acceptance and unconditional love. So 'B', very slowly and gently approach 'A', and, attuning to him or her, silently ask permission to establish contact. Very gently, very carefully, very slowly, 'B', then begin to unfold 'A' in as reassuring a manner as possible to the most open and free position you can imagine.

All the while, 'B', send your partner unconditional love, imagining yourself radiating it out as a beacon to him or her. 'A', you visualise yourself being filled with this light, cleansing and healing you as you are being unfolded.

'B', if you finish before the music ends, simply keep your hands on your partner reassuringly, stroking him or her if you wish, and continue to radiate love. When the music stops, gently help the person to get up and quietly reverse roles without speaking. You will have time to talk about your experience with the exercise later. Are there any questions? Ready. Begin.

(If using other music, allow 3-5 minutes for each partner. When everyone is finished, give participants time to talk about their experience with this exercise, or simply to be with each other in the silence.)

UNFOLDING (IN GROUPS)
(Close-Touching and Attunement Game)

(Suggested music: 'Heart Chakra' *by Joel Andrews. Review* 'Unfolding' (In Pairs) *on the preceding page. Instead of two people working together, divide into groups of from three to six people, depending upon how much time is available and how deep an experience you wish to give participants. Allow from five to twenty minutes for each participant. After demonstrating the first part of the regular 'Unfolding' process, continue with the following instructions.)*

Once you have the person unfolded, each member of the group attunes to discover what you can do to help the person to feel nurtured. It may be giving a head massage, or stroking the person's body lovingly. It may be giving a foot massage, or resting your head on the person's chest, or stroking the person's hair, or simply holding the person's hand and radiating loving, healing thoughts and feelings. Attune to the person to discover what the person would appreciate, and not simply what you want to do. Keep in physical contact with the person at all times.

When the time is up, gently help the person to get up. *Without any talking* the next person moves on to the floor, and the process continues until everyone has had a turn. This non-verbal game helps you attune to one another in complete silence. You will have time to talk about your experience with it later.

Are there any questions? Ready. Begin.

(When everyone is finished, invite participants to talk about their experience with the exercise, or simply to be with each other in the silence.)

WHAT I LOVE ABOUT MYSELF*
(Exploration Game)

Form groups of three, preferably with people you do not know very well. Decide who is 'A', 'B' and 'C', and sit quietly facing each other.

Most people are conditioned as children not to talk about themselves and their sense of self-worth. Parents, teachers and others say it is impolite, conceited, immodest, even arrogant to do so. But honest self-appraisal and genuine self-appreciation are quite different from bragging or boasting. The injunction 'Know thyself' surely means to recognise and accept both your strengths and your weaknesses, your 'positive' qualities as well as your 'negative' ones, your assets as well as your liabilities, and to be able to talk about them simply, clearly and objectively.

This exercise helps to counteract that childhood conditioning and affirm the love you must have for yourself if you are to be able to love anyone else.

So now for the next few moments, 'A', you tell 'B' and 'C' what you love about *yourself*. It is not to be a list of things you love *about life,* such as chocolate, dogs, roses, Mozart and the colour blue, but rather a long list of what you love *about yourself.*

'B' and 'C', *without responding in any way,* you give your full attention and support to 'A', maintaining eye contact with 'A' at all times, and, if you wish, holding hands, so as to provide contact, safety and trust for the three of you. After a few minutes, I will say, "Stop," and without discussion 'B', you and later 'C' then start. The purpose of this game is to get in touch with your own habits, skills, qualities, values, feelings, ideas and other so-called 'good points' and to express them freely to others. Are there any questions? Ready. Begin.

(When everyone is finished, invite participants to talk about their experience with the exercise, either with their partners or in the group.)

*From *Bringing More Love Into Your Life: The Choice Is Yours* by Eileen Caddy and David Earl Platts, Ph.D. ISBN 0-905249-75-5

WHAT IS YOUR NEXT STEP?
(Exploration Game)

(Everyone needs pen and paper for this exercise which easily lends itself to relating to the theme or purpose of the group. For example, tailor it to the group by asking, "To bring more play into your life, what is your next step?" "To empower yourself, what is your next step?" or "To heal yourself, what is your next step?" In addition, you may use this exercise with totally different questions, such as "Who are you?" or "What gift do you have to give?")

Choose a partner, decide who is 'A' and who is 'B', and sit quietly facing each other. Take pen and paper with you.

'A' is the scribe first, so you take the paper from 'B' which you will return to 'B' later. 'B', close your eyes, take several deep breaths, and then move into a quiet frame of mind, releasing all thoughts and feelings, and letting your own deep sense of Self take over. Do not try to force anything to happen. Do not try to think about anything. Just allow whatever comes to you to come spontaneously, without any concern or judgment about it.

When 'B' is relaxed, 'A', you ask 'B' by name the question, " (Name) , what is your next step?" And whatever comes, 'B', you repeat it aloud. It is to be a word, a short phrase, or no more than one simple sentence. This exercise is not meant to elicit any long explanation, description or dialogue.

'A', you then write down the response, after which 'A', you again ask 'B', " (Name) , what is your next step?" 'B', you then allow another response to come and say it aloud which 'A', you then write down, and so on and on until the time is up. If 'B' feels stuck with no responses coming, 'A', you continue to repeat the question every few seconds until a response does come.

Are there any questions? Ready. Begin. 'B', find a comfortable position, close your eyes and take several deep breaths. And now 'A', begin to ask your partner, " (Name) , what is your next step?"'

(Pause 5-10 minutes for the responses to come, the longer the better, as deeper, more meaningful responses often come with greater time. Then continue with the following instructions.)

Finish the response you are doing now and then stop. 'A', you sign your name and date your record of 'B's responses, indicating you have recorded your partner's responses accurately as you heard them. 'B', you may now open your eyes. 'A', read the responses which 'B' has given you, and 'B', open yourself completely to re-absorb these responses which came from within yourself.

(Pause 1-2 minutes, then continue with the following instructions.)

Now 'A', you return the paper to 'B'. *Without talking,* reverse roles. 'B', you take the paper belonging to 'A'. 'A', close your eyes and take several deep breaths. 'B', begin to ask your partner, " (Name) , what is your next step?"

(Pause 5-10 minutes, then continue with the following instructions.)

Finish the response you are doing now and then stop. 'B', sign your name and date your record of 'A's responses. 'A', you may now open your eyes. 'B', read the responses which 'A' has made, and 'A', open yourself completely to re-absorb these responses which came from within yourself.

(Pause 1-2 minutes, then continue with the following instructions.)

Now form a circle. Read through your list of possible next steps, and mark each one you are willing to commit yourself to taking within the next seven days.

(Pause 1-2 minutes, then continue with the following instructions.)

Each person may now tell the group in *one* sentence, *one* step you are sincerely committing yourself to take within the next seven days.

(When everyone is finished, invite participants to talk about their experience with the exercise.)

CHART 1 PRIMARY USES OF EXERCISES AND GAMES

EXERCISES & GAMES	Preparing the Group	Opening Games	Name Games	Action Games	Silly Games	Creative Games	Trust Games	Close-Touching Games	Exploration Games	Attunement Games	Closing Games
Ally Exercise	•										
Animal Identification									•		
Appreciation Circle 1											•
Appreciation Circle 2											•
Appreciation Circle 3											•
Blind Sculptor							•	•			
Camera Walk							•		•		
Car Car							•	•			
Car Wash							•	•			
Caterpillar					•			•			
Choosing a Leader						•			•		
Circle Pass					•						
Cows and Ducks					•		•				
Cradle Rock							•	•			
Creating Your Reality									•		
Cup Massage							•	•			
Elephants' Scratch					•			•			
Elephant Walk							•			•	
Energy Creation					•	•					
Everybody Is It				•	•						
Evocation of Openness							•		•		
Expectations	•										
Eye Contact									•		
Fairies and Dragons					•				•		
Fountain of Love									•	•	
Free Association									•		
Frozen Tag				•	•						
Greeting Dance		•									
Group Agreements	•										
Group Knot									•	•	
Group Spiral									•		•
Group Story						•				•	

EXERCISES & GAMES	Preparing the Group	Opening Games	Name Games	Action Games	Silly Games	Creative Games	Trust Games	Close-Touching Games	Exploration Games	Attunement Games	Closing Games
Hand Communication							•			•	
Head and Shoulders etc				•	•						
Hug Tag				•	•						
Human Spring							•			•	
Humless					•		•				
I Bless You, I Trust You										•	•
Ice-Breaker	•		•								
I Imagine	•									•	
Lap Sit							•	•			
Learning to See Others									•	•	
Meditation Dance										•	•
Mirroring						•				•	
Morning Routine					•	•					
Moving Statues						•				•	
Name Chain		•	•								
Name Mantra		•	•								
Nicknames			•						•		
People Pass							•	•			
People-to-People					•			•			
Personal Introductions	•										
Picture Post Cards						•			•		
Pillow Toss		•	•								
Planets							•			•	•
Prui					•		•				
Rain										•	
Sensuality Walk							•		•		
Sentence Completion				•	•						
Shoulder Massage							•	•			
Stand Up							•			•	
Trust Fall							•	•			
Trust Walk							•				
Unfolding (Pairs)								•		•	
Unfolding (Groups)								•		•	
What I Love									•		
What Is Your Next Step									•		

RECOMMENDED READING

NEW GAMES

These books are collections of new games, that is, games which everyone can play, which are safe, which foster cooperation rather than competition and which are good recreational fun. If any of these books should become out-of-print, it would be well worth looking for them in second-hand book shops.

- *The Cooperative Sports & Games Book, Challenge Without Competition,* by Terry Orlick. New York: Pantheon Books.
- *The New Games Book* and *More New Games Book,* edited by Andrew Fluegelman and Shoshana Tembeck. New York: Doubleday and Company.
- *New Games For the Whole Family,* by Dale N. LeFevre. New York: Perigee Books.

PSYCHOSYNTHESIS

Several *Playful Self-Discovery* exercises and games come from psychosynthesis, a holistic educational and psychospiritual approach to human growth and development. The following books (some of which are available in other languages in addition to English) offer many self-help techniques and exercises designed to increase self-understanding, self-acceptance and self-mastery.

- *Bringing More Love Into Your Life: The Choice Is Yours,* by Eileen Caddy and David Earl Platts, Ph.D. Forres, Scotland: Findhorn Press.
- *Growing Whole: Self-Realization on an Endangered Planet,* by Molly Young Brown. Center City, Minnesota: Hazelden Books.
- *Psychosynthesis: A Manual of Principles and Techniques,* by Roberto Assagioli, M.D. Wellingborough, England: Crucible.
- *What We May Be: The Vision and Techniques of Psychosynthesis,* by Piero Ferrucci. Wellingborough, England: Crucible.

ABOUT THE FINDHORN FOUNDATION

The Findhorn Foundation is a charitable trust and an international spiritual community in northeast Scotland. Founded in 1962 near the village of Findhorn by Eileen and Peter Caddy and Dorothy Maclean, it comprises a central core of people who live and work together, as well as a wider community who share its values and vision.

First known for its work with plants and communication with the nature realms, it has since become a centre for spiritual and holistic education as well. Its programmes and publications are based on the same attunement to Spirit evidenced in its early work with nature.

While it has no formal doctrine or creed, the Findhorn Foundation holds that an evolutionary expansion of consciousness is creating new patterns of civilisation infused with spiritual values. This expansion has its divine source centred within each human being, accessible directly through prayer, meditation and other spiritual disciplines.

The Findhorn Foundation encourages the taking of individual initiative and responsibility while drawing upon the support and synergy of group living. It holds that work is love in action, and fosters service and synthesis on both personal and planetary levels. It celebrates the intelligence, interconnectedness, love, sacredness, unity and wholeness of all life.

People who live in the community seek to embody and express these principles in daily life. They offer a regular programme of short courses and conferences reflecting their ideals to the thousands of guests who visit throughout the year to participate in the life of the community.

For further information, a list of books, audio tapes and videos is available from Findhorn Press, The Park, Findhorn, Forres IV36 0TZ, Scotland, and a Guest Programme brochure is available from the Accommodations Secretary, Cluny Hill College, Forres IV36 0RD, Scotland.

ABOUT THE AUTHOR

David Earl Platts, Ph.D. has been teaching and leading groups internationally for many years. He is a popular management consultant, trainer, writer, speaker and counsellor, and travels widely each year giving lectures and courses.

Dr. Platts directs his own personal and professional development consultancy and has a private counselling practice. He specialises in psychosynthesis, a holistic educational and psychospiritual approach to human growth and development. He also is a member of the adjunct faculty of Cluny Hill College in Scotland.

For eight years he was a staff member of the Findhorn Foundation, where he directed the *Group Discovery* programme upon which this book is based, served as an adult education advisor and trainer and co-authored, produced and directed a number of audio cassette tapes on personal development themes with Eileen Caddy, one of the Foundation's founders.

Dr. Platts went on to compile and edit a book of her inspirational guidance, *Opening Doors Within,* now published in more than a dozen languages. Later they collaborated to write *Bringing More Love Into Your Life: The Choice Is Yours,* a workbook based upon a seven-day residential course they presented at the Foundation for many years. It was followed by *Choosing To Love,* an edited version of principles and techniques from their workbook.

He later compiled and published the *International Psychosynthesis Directory,* listing from 31 countries 650 centres, groups and individuals who work with the principles and methods of psychosynthesis.

Dr. Platts makes himself available as a consultant, lecturer and trainer to individuals, groups and organisations. His work enhances people's awareness of themselves and their potential and provides a balance of theory and practice within a relaxed, supportive environment. He tailors his work to meet the special interests and needs of clients and programme organisers. He may be contacted care of Findhorn Press, The Park, Findhorn, Forres IV36 0TZ, Scotland.